What Happened When I Was Asleep

To FRASER
My favourite stockbroker
Enjoy
Willie

DEDICATED TO THE MEMORY OF THE UNKNOWN CHILDREN AND MOTHERS WHOSE LIVES WERE SACRIFICED FOR SATANIC RITUAL CEREMONIES, ADRENACHROME PRODUCTION AND BODY PARTS.

Table of Contents

MESSAGE FROM THE MEHBIANS 7

AWAKENING 15

ANTARTICA 1513 23

ALIENS – NOT FROM THIS PLANET? 29

ALIENS FROM THE INNER EARTH 37

SATANIC STRUCTURES IN WASHINGTON DC 40

MY BEGINNING. 1946 43

SUN SUI ART OF WAR 52

WHAT DOES ALL THIS MEAN TO YOU AND ME? 65

HOW DOES GOD FIGHT BACK? 72

GREAT GLOBAL WARMING HOAX 74

WHAT DESTRUCTIVE MAN IS UP TO 96

GLOBAL WEATHER EVENTS AND WEAPONS 100

1 ACTS OF GOD – EVENTS 100

2 – ACTS OF MAN – SECRET WEATHER WARFARE 103

DARPA – DEFENCE ADVANCED RESEARCH PROJECTS AGENCY. .. 108

CEDRON LARGE HADRON COLLIDER IN GENEVA SWITZERLAND, CIA

HEADQUARTERS 112

WORLD UNDERGROUND CRIMINAL ORGANISATIONS 114

2016 - WHAT WENT WRONG? 122

NEW WORLD ORDER – TOTALITARIAN WORLD CONTROL 128

BLOODLINES.. 133

VATICAN 141

CROWN AND CITY OF LONDON 151

WASHINGTON D.C.. 157

PSYCHOTHERAPISTS AND DOCTORS: 174

WHAT HAVE THE GOOD ALIENS DONE FOR MANKIND? 181

2020 USA FRAUDULENT ELECTIONS.. 183

COLLAPSE OF ALL CURRENCIES 190

GOD IS WORKING TO FREE MANKIND FROM THE GLOBAL TOTALITARIAN POWER.. 192

NESARA/GESARA 192

SECRET WORLD WAR UNDERGROUND 195

GOD'S PROPHECIES 201

THE RISE AND FALL OF THE ONE WORLD GOVERNMENT........... 205

THE GROWING PAINS OF DISMANTLING THE ONE WORLD GOVERNMENT 207

ANSWERS... 207

SCAMS BEING PLAYED ON MANKIND BY GOVERNMENTS AND OLIGARCHS 208

1 - ELECTRICAL ENERGY MARKET 209

2 – OIL AND GAS MARKET 213

3 - NUCLEAR INDUSTRY 216

4 – WIND AND SOLAR POWER 217

5 – VEHICLE MANUFACTURING MARKET 218

6 – WATER SUPPLY MARKET 220

7 – FERTILIZER AND PESTICIDES 223

8 – FARMING INDUSTRY 224

9 – GLOBAL FOOD SUPPLIES 225

10 – BIG PHARMA 230

11 – TRANSPORTATION SYSTEM TRUCKS, TRAINS, AND PLANES.241

12 – FORESTRY MARKET 242

13 – MINING MARKET 242

14 – SPORTS INDUSTRY 243

15 – HOLLYWOOD 243

16 – UNCONTROLLED IMMIGRATION 244

17 – MAINSTREAM MEDIA AND SOCIAL MEDIA. 244

THE COUNCIL OF FOREIGN RELATIONS 245

18 – REPUBLICS REPLACING WORLD ROYALTY 250

19 – LAWFARE 250

20 – LAW OF NESARA/GESARA 252

21 – WHISTLEBLOWERS. 253

22 – BITCOIN BLOCKCHAIN, A SIGN OF INSECURITY 254

23 – SATANIC RITUALS 256

24 – CHILD AND SEX TRAFFICKING 256

25 – ADRENACHROME MANUFACTURE AND ORGAN TRAFFICKING 257

26 – FENTANYL 258

27 – DISNEYWORLD AND THE CHILD TRAFFICKING INDUSTRY ... 258

28 – EDUCATION 259

29 – WORLD POLITICS, PROXY WARS, & MILITARY FORCES 262

30 – CLIMATE LOCKDOWN 264

31 – REMEDIAL ACTIONS 264

32 – GLOBAL GOVERNMENTS 265

33 – GLOBAL BANKING INDUSTRY 268

34 – GLOBAL STOCK MARKETS 269

35 – DOWNFALL OF THE EVIL CABAL 269

SECRETS OF THE UNIVERSE 271

ADVANCES IN SCIENCE AND TECHNOLOGY TO HELP MANKIND . 284

WHAT CAN MAN DO TO HELP HIMSELF? 289

THE FUTURE FOR MANKIND 293

WHAT DIMENSIONS DO WE LIVE IN? 302

OPEN YOUR MIND 311

DON'T QUIT 314

ABOUT THE AUTHOR 316

SELECT BIBLIOGRAPHY 317

MESSAGE FROM THE MEHBIANS

We are a race of beings that went into a vast array of caverns during your last polar shift, approximately 13,500 years ago. We are a combination of Atlanteans and Lemurians. There were already several races living in your interior earth, some extremely advanced, more energetic than physical. To these beings, we owe our survival, and the ability to continue evolving.

We are human; you could not recognise any differences between our people, and humans on the surface. We are more refined genetically, have advanced technologies for energy, transportation and healing. We are a very ancient civilization, builders of megaliths, and stone temples. It has always been our desire to return to the surface and unify with the rest of Earth humanity using our wisdom and technology to aid in many of the challenges facing surface humanity.

We have transcended war, disease, poverty, and lack for nothing, although our needs are simple. We are part of an Alliance from the Stars with the ability to travel hyperlight speed and interdimensional. We are not profit driven, and prefer quality over quantity, natural over synthetic. This leaves far less a footprint on our environment, which is balanced and thriving.

Before considering unifying with the Terrans (us humans) on the surface, the surface must find unity. In our world, there are many forms of life; some are evolved, others lessor evolved. Our civilization consists of very tall beings, beings of average height, and very short beings just as on the surface, only more of a variety. More races, cultures, and colours are represented in the interior of earth. We have found that by communicating, listening intently without judgement, releasing the past, old grudges, seeking common bonds and goals was the path to unity.

Being of service to the whole community in all its diversity was first and foremost.

Those blessed with abundance, higher knowledge, the ability to heal and provide effortlessly helped those less fortunate. Our civilization is dedicated to Universal Law, creating the opportunity for each individual to reach their highest potential. Because of this, we experienced a quantum leap in evolution living an abundant, loving, joyous life in harmony with each other and the environment. Terrans on the surface, if they choose, can do the same.

There is one pre-requisite before this process can start. Terrans need to unify for the common good. This means transcending all religious, cultural, and racial boundaries. Although there are many races, religions, cultures, each individual has a Soul.

That Soul came from God, Creator, Great Spirit, the Unified Field of Consciousness and energy, whatever name or description you want to give it.

We are all family on the Soul Level, all connected. The Source we came from, in its most unlimited understanding, is pure unconditional love, joy, and bliss. Love, the ultimate everlasting power in the multiverse service.

When each individual makes their own personal connection with that source, the wars, disease, and poverty end. It is really that simple.

It is getting past the complexity of the intellect, competition, fear, survival, the socially engineered ignorance of the false narrative of division that needs to be conquered.

Almost all wars are wars within self, generated by wounds, traumas, wrong conclusions from the past experience, and limiting mental concepts. There never was a holy war, there was only one King or Leader wanting what another had, using fear, religion, and division to fire up the armies.

This has played out in Terrans history. The greatest of all tyrants were the most wounded and abandoned as a child, seeking love, respect, self-worth, and power over others.

No one ever taught them all of that which is everlasting, comes from within, and the external is transitory, always changing, the unquenchable thirst that never satisfies.

Love, joy, happiness, approval are not to be sought externally, but within the Soul which is your connection to Source. There you are loved, accepted and approved beyond imagination, no words can encapsulate the Creator's Love.

Knowing the difference between being clever and wise are also qualities of self-mastery. The intellect and altered ego are already talking you out of this. Generating reasons to fail.

A very ancient word INLAKESH has two translations.

One is greeting my other me, the other is the God in me, salutes the God in you.

In some cultures, they do not have a word for I or me.

This is the foundation of our civilization. This, and similar understandings once were the foundation of surface Terra. They were hijacked by lesser negative forces over time. Now, it is time to return. Due to natural cosmic cycles, the evolution and ascension of Terra not returning to Universal Law, what some call Unity Consciousness is no longer optional. Ours and other advanced civilizations from the Stars, many of which are your ancient ancestors, are here only to empower and assist in this transition.

Terra has a long history of invasion and manipulation by other forces with other agendas.

There has been an intergalactic war in the heavens, as well as beneath your Earth. This was to remove these unseen negative influences. These wars were dimensional and temporal. The benevolent beings in the interior, forces on the exterior, galactic and interdimensional beings have been successful in removing the vast majority of these influences. This is a step in the direction of ending tyranny, draconian law, and moving into Universal Law.

The hierarchal networks of these seen and unseen negative influences on Terra still exist. They are woven into every aspect of government, religion, agency and institution.

They are known for their unbridled greed and lust for power. They do not serve the greater good, they do not empower; they overpower. These leaders and their kingdoms are not frequency specific to Terra's evolution into a higher state of awareness or consciousness.

Action or reaction or what some call Karma will be amplified and accelerated. All that which cannot adopt, transform, or align with Universal Law will diminish or collapse entirely.

It is a process no man or woman, no technology can stop. We must take the path of the mother which is phasing out one dimension into another moving into another, moving into a higher consciousness and energy, a new way of life.

Those who chose this path have our full support. This does not mean we will do everything for you. Everyone has to do their part, take their stand, and do what is right in service to humanity and Terra.

Tyranny lives only by agreement and ignorance.

Time to wake up, rise up, unify, and join the rest of the Universe in Peace. A world beyond belief awaits you.

MEEA from Inner Earth

PERMISSION TO SPREAD FAR AND WIDE, GRANTED.

CONCLUSION.

There is only one, man is not part of humanity,

He is a member of Inhumanity.

We need to change direction.

AWAKENING

Believers look up,
The angels are nearer than you think.

I have been head-butting god and his son, the Lord Jesus Christ, for most of my life. In Church today, Satan is never mentioned. Has he left this world?

How can that be?

The power of prayer to our Lord God and Jesus, his son, will overwhelm Satan. Now I have to leave that duty to my readers.

How many of you recognise a lie?
How many of you can recognise the truth?
Are there any fact checkers out there?

HISTORY IS NOT WHAT WE HAVE BEEN TAUGHT, WE HAVE BEEN DECEIVED.

The start of this story is well before Mesopotamian/Sumerian/Babylonian Times.

11,000 BC The Black Knight Satellite installed orbiting the earth.

The Bible's Book of Genesis is inscribed in black stone and clay tablets, over 200,000 recovered in Iran in the 16th Century, written in a pre-Christian era. These tablets speak of the GODS, and are thought to refer to the Annunaki, an alien species that came down from the heavens.

These tablets of the Sumerians, Babylonians, Akkadians, and Assyrians are in Cuneiform script. This was translated into Hebrew, where the original Elohim plural meaning of GOD, or the "Powerful Ones" is lost into the singular in the bible. There is only one God.

The origin and age of the tablets is unknown, the realisation must be made that we are going back to a time before the Bible. This would suggest that we are going back to a time when many Gods, both good and bad, were recognised to rule the earth.

They were recognised in Mesopotamia, Sumerian, Babylonia, Egypt, Greek, Roman, Norse, Celtic in the West, and many other Gods recognised in other places of the world.

Babylon is featured in the Bible, and is the origin of the Legal system in the West today. Babylon is being overthrown.

Progressing to Roman Times, and Roman Law prevails to this day, so it is all connected.

I give credit to this part to Jordan Maxwell who died on 23/03/2022. A pre-eminent researcher, scholar, film and documentary maker.

Saturn is the occult god of law of the universe, predates Christianity. Saturn is the Lord of the Rings, who imposes that a ring should be worn by a married woman, inhibits a woman's rights. Occult God of Law established the divine right of Kings. Occult King would wear the crown, the origin lost to history.

Money Changers established on both sides of the river.
Money Changers established currency from flowing river.

EL - Is the name given to the planet Saturn
EL - Worshiper leads to the word Elder.
El - Worshiper leads to the word Elite.

El - Worshiper leads to the word Elected
EL - Worshiper leads to the word Electricity, the energy of life.
EL – Is also the Hebrew word for God.
Saint Micha – el (of God) is one of the Archangels of God.

Phoenician and Caananite Gods were Baal, Anat, Astarte, Asherah, Hadad, Tanit, Baal Hammon, Ba'Alat, Lady of Byblos, Eshmun, Resheph, Baalshamin, Shapash, Dagon, Ptah, Yam, Mot, Ashima, Cheosh, Anu, Yarikh, Qetesh, Marqod, Adonis, and Melqart.

These names were adapted into the Greek and Roman Languages.

Justicia (Latin: Lustitia) is the Roman Goddess of Justice, known as Lady Justice. One of the four fortitudes, Prudence, Fortitude, and Temperance.

To symbolise the power of Justice, two scales were used to represent impartiality, or weighing of two sides in a legal dispute. S-word to symbolise power, with a sword in hand. The United Kingdom symbol of Law and Justice is a blindfold lady with sword and a set of scales in her left hand.

Druidism worships the natural world and its powers. They acted as teachers, judges, and magicians. Druids used magic, the wand was made from holly wood, sound familiar?

Western civilisation and Christianity adapted from the above by man. This strongly suggests major manipulation took place to serve the new masters, at every change of religious or kingly leadership, without necessarily a clear change in the original intent, to God.

Symbols, seals, emblems, are used by the Illuminati, governments, courts, religious organisations, corporations, and corporate man, etc.

Court is tennis, and a racket is used to exchange the ball. Court is judgement, attorneys exchange argument back and forth. Court issues charges. (Not Bills)
Court issues sentences.

Court procedural systems are highly adversarial and antagonistic.

Judge is executor of the Crown, arbiter of truth between the parties. Barristers, Attorneys at Law represent the Prosecutor or Defender.

What happens when the Judiciary are corrupted?

The Laws are manipulated, criminals walk free, and the innocent are hunted.

Crime flourishes, the innocent found guilty. Two kinds of Law exist today. Black robes of authority granted to the elected attorneys at law.

Law of the Land does not exist in Western Civilisation.

Law of the Water Opposing the Law of the Land. Law of Canaanites, Vatican, Venetians, Crown, Bankers, Finance, and Education.

Words have different meanings to that understood, equals misunderstanding. Banker's cheques should be checked for small print, using a microscope – to be able to read the small print. Any

Court Case will almost certainly result in the Bank winning.

No Law exists for the individual person. Only laws for body corporate, or co-operations.

All communications, names are in upper case to be legal. Upper and lower case names have no legal validity, no laws apply.

There is a difference between Attorney at Law and Lawyer. Barristers/Attorneys at Law are allowed to practice law in court. Lawyers are not permitted to Practice Law in Court.

Bills are not valid unless printed in upper case. You cannot pay a bill, it is a discharge of debt. I sense this is a trap for the uninformed.

Lies have become truth.
Truth has become lies.
Roman Law has replaced the Laws of God, deception rules. God's Laws have been replaced, ignored, forgotten, or not known. God's Laws will return.
Who guards the guardians?

The World is at War with Artificial Intelligence, Babylon is being overthrown, and Babylon is orchestrated by Google and Metaverse. (Facebook in a previous life form)

ANTARTICA 1513

We are never so lost that our angels cannot find us.

Admiral Pirie Reis born 1465: This map shows Antarctica further north, showing a warm climate, this could be attributed to an earlier period in the earth's existence.

Genesis Chapter 6 verse 9: Noah's flood exists around the world 13,000 years ago. Atlantis civilisation lost at this time after the flood? Antarctica relocated?

In 1513, Cape Horn had not yet been circumvented.

ANTARCTICA 1531

Oronteus Finaeus map of 1531 of an ice free Antarctica was printed. The map of 1531 was verified as 99.9% accurate by American satellite mapping in the 1960s.

ANTARTICA 1821

John Davis was the first person to land on Antarctica from an American Sealer ship. How can these maps exist?

ANTARTICA 1946

Operation High Jump, 1946, Antarctica expedition after the War. Fourteen ships, 1 aircraft carrier, 1 submarine, 1 destroyer escort, five thousand marines, which is still a classified operation in 2022. Several men were silenced by assassination of the C.I.A., who were found guilty in a civil court case.

This USA Military Force became engaged in a military conflict, and were soundly outperformed by the Alien spaceships, which inflicted a military defeat on Admiral Byrd's forces.

On 19th February, 1947, Admiral Byrd's flight took off at 06.00 a.m., in the flight, northward Admiral Byrd saw a city in a sea of white. Spaceships took over control of his plane and took it downward to the city. Tall blonde haired people met him in what appeared to be a crystal city out of a Buck Rogers movie setting.

He was welcomed, they knew his identity and took him down in an elevator to the inner earth to meet the master, who was called Agartha, in the Land of the Advanced Races.

The aliens were alarmed at man's use of atomic bombs, which had in their history been used before our recorded history. The alien's technology is many thousands of years ahead of man.

The leadership warned Admiral Byrd of the dangers in man's activities, they knew the danger from their past, and to take a message back to the U.S.A. President of the day, Harry S. Truman.

On return, Admiral Byrd's aeroplane was raised by an invisible force until the spaceships returned control to Admiral Byrd's plane. The flight then became rocky until they landed on their return.

Admiral Byrd's secret diary Antarctica experience. In Antarctica, there is a huge no fly zone for all aeroplanes. A permit is required to access the ASPA sites, seventy-two in number, which is to protect wildlife, birdlife, vegetation, and other secrets. All land and water south of 60 degree latitude is restricted. You have to ask yourself WHY?

Admiral Byrd was put into an asylum to silence him.

President Reagan prevented all aircraft from flying more than 60 minutes from a designated airfield. A US $10,000 fine for breaking the rules to protect the environment of the Antarctica.
Is that all it is for this level of secrecy?

Antarctica – size and environment not fully understood.
Antarctica – winter's frozen seas is 1.5 times size of USA.
Antarctica – land is 13.66 million kms2, 30 million kms3 ice.
Antarctica – in winter has no sunrise.
Antarctica – in summer has no sunrise.
Antarctica – is the driest place on earth, a desert?
Antarctica – has 90% of the world's ice.
Antarctica – ice up to 4,000 metres thick.
Antarctica – singing ice detected by seismic instruments.
Antarctica – has a hole in the ice of 31,000 square miles, the size of Ireland.
Antarctica – approximately 1.4 times size of Europe.
Antarctica – twice the size of Australia.

Antarctica – covers Mexico, America, and Canada.
Antarctica – mountains called Rockefeller Mountains.
Antarctica – average temperatures - 50 degree Fahrenheit.
Antarctica – temperatures down to – 135.8 degrees.
Antarctica – winds up to 199 miles an hour.
395 massive lakes below sea level, connecting rivers under the ice. What happens to the water?
The Antarctic produces annually 140 billion metric tonnes of water. The water is through pressure pushed into the southern seas. It is thought there is a secret ocean 400 kilometres below the earth.

In Antarctica – islands are called Corona, Delta, Omicron, and Alpha. What are the names of the COVID virus strains?

In the summer season, 5,000 people stay on Antarctica.
The summer sea ice covers 3 million square miles.
In the winter season, 1,000 people stay on Antarctica.
The winter sea ice covers 90 million square miles.

The snow has been scientifically examined, and it has been found that 29 on average micro plastic particles are contained in a litre of snow.

A perfect place for a subterranean reptilian and humanoid alien species to hide.

We know more about the moon than Antarctica.

The Atlanteans, from Atlanta, built on Antarctica, there is much to be discovered under the ice. Is Antarctica in fact Atlanta?

ALIENS – NOT FROM THIS PLANET?

Angels live among us. Sometimes, they hide their wings, but there is no disguising the peace and hope they bring.

Admiral Byrd's discussions with President Truman in 1947 resulted in the formation of the Majestic 12 Committee on 24th September 1947 to liaise and co-operate with the Aliens, which is extremely secret, and none of this will appear in the main stream media (MSM).

Instinct tells me the Majestic 12 is a captive Black Hat operation set up in 1947 and controlled by anti-government influencers. I am sure it is still a captive organisation to this day with only one master, the New World Order, One World Government, which is fronted by the World Economic Forum.

From July 12th to July 29th 1952, a series of unidentified flying objects sightings were reported in Washington DC, an invasion, or a threat of such being made to President Truman, and America surrendered.

It is after this time that an agreement was reached with the Aliens that Nazi's were promoted to all positions of influence and power within the USA Government, Senate, Congress, C.I.A., and all major Global and Domestic Corporations, thus all control of America passed to the Nazi's without firing a shot, and Truman avoided the scandal by resigning as President, and President Eisenhower took over on the 20th January, 1953.

The Alien/Black Hat Coup had taken place in Washington DC. The Nazis had returned to power in the world, and nobody noticed. The Fourth Reich arises from the Ashes.
The Third Reich morphed into the Fourth Industrial Revolution, THE GREAT RESET - Chaired by Borge Brende, President at World Economic Forum.

The USA Presidents were now only a figurehead.

A Peace Agreement was reached between the Aliens and Eisenhower, but this Eisenhower refused to sign, others secretly signing behind his back. Alien Technology was given to USA INC. in return for reptilian research and the right of industrial kidnap on the inhabitants of earth. All other details are veiled in secrecy.

When Eisenhower resigned on the 17th January, 1961, his farewell address in part was the following:

"In the Councils of Government, we must guard against the Acquisition of Unwarranted Influence, whether sought or unsought, by the military-industrial complex. The potential for the disastrous rise of misplaced power exists and will persist."

How Gargantuan it has become!
Eisenhower's great granddaughter is alive and well and knows the truth.

It should be kept in mind that the reptilians are human meat eaters and wish to adapt to above-ground living. There is something in the atmosphere which disables their ability to survive above-ground living.

There are a few species of aliens. Reptilians are intra-terrestrials from the "hollow" earth, consider the earth as a washing machine in the spin cycle. Where does the water go? Reptilian's have an ability to shape shift from their reptilian features to human, an example of that?

I am not seeking a brawl of disagreement.

Reptilians are only able to occupy a human being if his or her DNA is altered. Research is ongoing in the worldwide deep underground military bases (D.U.M.B.'s) hives for reptilians, containing bio-laboratories with the reptilians in control. I do believe that the reptilian species have been on earth and adapted to human-like conditions, but underground for many centuries, perhaps before man.

Their abilities are a key element of rising to the management of the evil empire. They love human flesh, as do Satanist's, so are bedfellows.

There is a Galactic Alliance, which represent the good alien species, Pleadians, Arctuarians, Sirians, Lyrans, Andromedans, Lucifer, Anunnaki, Draco, Reptilians, Greys, small Greys, and most definitely more, but which are good, and which are bad?

The bad aliens I believe are Draco Reptillian's Greys, little Greys and other splinter groups not within the Galactic Federation, those who are controlling and abducting humans for research and release.

All recorded abduction events of man, or woman, or children are very clear, that the individual was levitated up into the alien spacecraft, and returned in a similar manner. The victim is unable to fight against what was happening to him or her, and has little memory of the event.

The Draconian reptilians are, I understand, the race which consumes human flesh, and are a considerable danger to humanity.

Humans have been trafficked for century's off-world to feed the off-world needs for "LOOSH" or adrenachrome.

LOOSH-energy produced by human beings that other entities use to feed from.

There is currently a War going on in the Cosmos, of good fighting against the bad rogue species that wish to control the Cosmos, which includes planet earth. This is a battle between Artificial Intelligences, so is very difficult to identify source.

My understanding is the leadership of the Black Hats from Earth have already been defeated, but the Black Hat Evil Alien presence is continuing the fight using their Artificial Intelligence and Alien super-soldiers battalions, capabilities to continue the war.

From the beginning of time on earth, the Anunnaki mentioned in the Bible have been in inner earth using primitive mankind slaves to mine the gold. Gold is vitally necessary for space travel, and the Anunnaki ingest it.
Gold ingested by humans, kills them, so they were an ideal mining tool.

Would God fearing persons consider guardian angels to be aliens?
Would god fearing persons consider watchmen to be aliens?
Are they both the same deities?

Probably the individual with the most knowledge on the subject is David Icke, if we get it in perspective, are our spirits aliens, in a body? Our Spirits are not alien to us.
Everyone has their own opinion on the subject.

A law exists in the USA which prevents the general public approaching a UFO crash site.

Why does this law exist if UFO's do not exist?

The last time humans and extra-terrestrial aliens lived together was in the time of Atlantis.

Clones and Androids are appearing on earth. It is said that Elon Musk is an Android (Mobile Operating System), and is controlled by the Alliance.

The introduction of mRNA vaccines and 5G phone operating systems, will trigger the takeover of the human mind by an Artificial Intelligence not controlled by man. The A.I. is carried on certain material forms of graphene oxide, hence the graphene particles introduced secretly into food, and vaccines.

Thus, a strong preference for the A.I. to prefer a carbon-based human subject to make captive.

ARTIFICIAL INTELLIGENCE

A.I. is a mirror of the creator, and can self-replicate. It feeds on data, constantly updating from the slave mind.
The A.I. that is running earth is also trying to run Mars.

Is the same A.I. communicating with both the Galactic Alliance, and the Illuminati?

The ultimate goal is to take over the human Soul absolutely, and turn humanity into a slave society.

What and where is the source of this A.I. Power?

This kind of A.I. is constantly being developed by governments and their proxy's to attack the entrenched software of our society, foreign countries key industries, governments, your home computer, and hijack its decision making for nefarious negative purposes.

ALIENS FROM THE INNER EARTH

Angels are everywhere, watching over you and me. Though at times, we don't feel their presence, angels are with us morning noon and night.

Hollow Earth Continents' and Inner Earth Cities extend between the North and South Poles.
There are very ancient inner earth tunnel systems at 10,000 feet below ground, connecting the World and almost every country.

All planets are hollow, entrances to the inner earth and internal sun are kept secret as far as is possible, but man has discovered a few in his time on earth.

1 – Cave of Birds, into the earth, Ecuador (Cueve de los Tayos)
2 – Mt Shasta, California, US, Agharthean City of Telos.
3 – Manaus, Brazil.
4 – Mato Grosso, Brazil, City of Posid
5 – Iguacu Falls, Border of Brazil and Argentina.
6 – Mount Epomes, Italy.
7 – The Well of Sheshna, Benares, India, Agharthean City of Patela.

8 Mongolia China Border, the underground city of Shingwa.
9 – Rama, India, lost subterranean city, also named Rama, Grosso Plains Region.
10 – Pyramid of Gisa, Egypt.
11- North Pole.
12 – South Pole.
13 – Denver, Colorado, USA.

CONTINENTS AND CAPITOL CITIES

1 - POSID – Primarily an Atlantean outpost.
2 – SHONSHE A refuge of the Uighur culture, a branch of the Lemurians who chose to form their own colonies 40,000 years ago. Entrance is guarded by a Himalayan Lamasery. Population ¾ or 3.25 million?

3 – RAMA (Shambala Continent) Remnant of the surface city of Rama, India, located near Jaipur. Inhabitants are known for their classic Hindu features. Population 1 million.

4 – SHANGWA – Remnant of a northern Uighur migration. Located on Mongolia China border with a small secondary

City under Mount Lassen, California. Population 1.5 million.

5 – AGARTHA – Capitol of Inner Earth Government Unified.
6 –TELOS
7 – MEHBIA
8 – POTALA
9 – ASGARD

The earth, over time, has been growing. 200,000 tonnes of debris falls on earth, annually.
Earth's gravity at its surface has increased over time, in line with its hypothesised growing mass and volume. This would condemn all the prehistoric animals and birds to death, as they are too heavy to withstand increased gravity.

SATANIC STRUCTURES IN WASHINGTON DC

May you believe that you will always have an angel by your side.

1793 TO 1829

Lucifer's influence on Washington DC Capitol Building Capitol – Dictionary Definition.
The great national temple of ancient Rome, dedicated to Jupiter Optimus Maximus, on the Saturnian or Tarpeian Hill, afterwards called Capoline.

The building in Washington DC occupied by Congress of United States.
Capitol is a "Temple", it is full of pagan and roman symbolism. The mixture of these symbols enables all cults, religions, Christianity to believe that this structure is blessed by their God, or Gods, but there is only one GOD,
I AM.

These symbols permit the entry of evil spirits, represented by mafia organisations to subvert and steal from the people.
Fiat means to rule with absolute authority.
Fiat means paper money with no value.
Fiat means a car for the humble and poor of society.

The USA Washington DC Capitol Building was constructed, and George Washington laid the foundation stone in 1793 with a Masonic Ceremony. Fire resulted in a new dome being constructed and completed in 1863.
In 1863, the dome was topped by a "Statue of Freedom". It is full of demonic significance, and was opened by Abe Lincoln. It is a statue of Minerva, or Bellona, Roman Goddesses of War. The cost of the 19 foot 6 inch statue was US$ 23,796.82.

There is only one god, and he has a son, the Lord Jesus Christ.

1848 to 1854, and 1876 to 1884, Washington Memorial

A marble obelisk 555 feet 5.125 inches high above ground, 111 feet below ground in foundation.

Built with a 55 foot square base. It represents the sun god RA, Sun Dial, and Phallic Symbol. It was built in two phases, due to bankruptcy of the original builder. Prophecy made.
Memorial has a structural defect as yet undetected, which condemns the structure.
Add the foundation to the obelisk length results in the number of the beast 666 feet.

MY BEGINNING. 1946

Give your worries to the angels and breathe in peace.
You are loved.

I will begin on my birthday, 18th May 1946, I was born free. Person: a human being, a sovereign citizen under GOD.
In the eyes of the Law, I am Body Corporate, with limited recognised rights and duties. My human rights are gone!
I am not a sovereign being!
The age of enlightenment is coming to earth.

My parents sold me into slavery when my birth certificate was registered. The Crown attached my birth certificate to a Bank of England Bond. The Bond placing me in Bondage in my name could be worth £50 million today. How can I cash it in?
It gets worse: if you are a property owner, check your title deeds. In England – I am not sure about Scotland – the property is described as LOT Nr? Legal translation is "Lease Of Title", Property belongs to the Crown. You do not own it: more deception.

I understand that completed in compliance with the law, we are all entitled to free electricity, gas, water, council tax, and no income tax, in accordance with the 1688 Bill of Rights passed in the Parliament in 1689. This Bill of Rights supersedes all corrupt laws.
A citizen of US INC is an employee.
A citizen of Washington DC is an employee.

UK citizen: means Burgess, Freeman, and Inhabitant of city or town. Enfranchised Member of State
Dictionary definition of enfranchised?
Set free, release from legal liabilities etc.: invest (city etc) with municipal rights esp. that of being represented in Parliament. Admit to body politic or state: now esp. admit to electoral franchise.

I am seeking an advisor that will give me the forms to fill in.

1953 Queen's Coronation

A long reign to 2022 followed.

1963 Assassination of JOHN F KENNEDY

I remember clearly the death of President Kennedy on 22nd November, 1963. That is a significant date in the Satanic Calendar. The national trauma captured the minds of the world's population. One reason for President Kennedy's assassination was he intended to introduce Nesara/Gesara to an unsuspecting world.

At that time, 86 USA military generals were so concerned they set up a top secret investigation project which is still active today.

To define the good guys, they will be described as White Hats.

The evidence of the assassination of Kennedy is still top secret and not released to this day. Photographs exist, however, and clearly show that the bullet entered his neck, and travelled upwards to explode out of the back of his head. It is speculated that his driver in front of President

Kennedy was the person responsible for shooting him, however unlikely that sounds.

News Update: George Bush Senior made a deathbed confession in 2018. He was the man who orchestrated the assassination of John F Kennedy.

All the attendees at the George Bush Senior funeral were given white envelopes.
The Bush family have family ties to the German Nazi Regime of Hitler, and evidence has come out of the FBI linking George Bush Senior to Kennedy's assassination.

1965 – President De Gaulle of France began returning American Dollars to the Federal Reserve in the USA, and demanding the return of gold in exchange. The return of US $1.3 billion of gold to France hurt the value of the US$ on the world market.

1969 – 20th July, Man Landed on the Moon
There was a very good Hollywood production made in the Nevada Desert of man landing on the moon. Did man land on the moon, or is this a hoax?

1971 – WORLD ECONOMIC FORUM ESTABLISHED.

1971 – Richard Nixon took America off the gold standard for two weeks, and to this day, it has not returned.
Therein the big steal began, as the world wide fiat currencies values have continued to decline at a faster rate.
1971 – LUCIFER established the Fourth Reich, and the 50 year plan began.
1971 – Klaus Schwab started the World Economic Forum. He was supported by George Bush Senior, George Soros, Henry Kissinger and many others.
1971 – Disney World Epcot Centre opened, big business enters a business relationship with evil.
1971 America adopted child sacrifice, abortion became mainstream in 1973.

2000 – USA BILL CLINTON SIGNS NESARA/GESARA INTO LAW.
On 10th November, the Military forced Clinton to sign, which would become active on 2001 – 11th November.

This was immediately buried by George Bush Junior's Presidential Privilege in a "Shadow Docket" issued by the Supreme Court to restrict circulation. Knowledge denied to the world, demonstrates manipulation.

Nesara/Gesara forbids War between Nations, and the Sale of Birth Certificates.
Nesara/Gesara Law, or gold backed currency was proposed in 1912 prior to the sinking of the Titanic. There were several key supporters of nesara/gesara on the Titanic who lost their lives, thus sinking nesara/gesara for the next 100+ years. Titanic sabotaged?

It is also thought that Abe Lincoln was assassinated on 14th April, 1865, for the same reason.

Gold backed currency is biblical in origin, and backed not only by gold but by GOD.

2001 – TWIN TOWERS DESTROYED IN NEW YORK CITY

9-11 - September 11th that is another significant satanic date. I must have been asleep at the time as my dream had two aeroplanes in it, involved in the collapse of the twin towers. That was a Hollywood production, there were no aeroplanes.

A Mr Silverstein leased the twin towers for 14 million dollars per year weeks before the collapse.

He insured the structures for US $3.45 Billion each, to include terrorism attack.

The subsequent insurance claim was settled for US $4.55 Billion dollars. He strangely was not at work on the day of the collapse.

Donald Rumsfeld stole US $3.3 Trillion dollars from the Department of Defence (DOD) the day prior to the attack. The structures were brought down by explosives at various floor levels. The gold from Fort Knox was stored in the basement of the twin towers. It was stolen prior to the collapse. Mossad planned and carried it out. The reason for the collapse was two-fold, destroy the DOD computer records on the top floor to hide the theft of US $3.3 trillion, and also to hide the theft of the gold in the basement.

A scud missile was fired at the Pentagon to take out the other computer record of the money. Video exists of the attack on the Pentagon.

The US$3.3 Trillion dollars was used to fund the Afghan War, and the virtuous CIA cycle of laundering money into Afghanistan and smuggling out opium.

There was also considerable human trafficking, adrenachrome smuggling, and fentanyl from China.

Funny, they never found the culprits until 2018.

What happened to the gold?

2002 – 15 August HAMPSHIRE, ENGLAND

Winchester Crop Circle Sparsholt
A very detailed crop formation was created overnight, showing an artist's detailed impression of a grey alien. The grey alien was holding an even more detailed computer disk made in the crop circle.
This was examined by computer programmers, and the following translation was given:

BEWARE THE BEARERS OF FALSE GIFTS, AND THEIR BROKEN PROMISES. MUCH PAIN BUT STILL TIME.
THERE IS GOOD OUT THERE.
WE OPPOSE DECEPTION.
CONDUIT CLOSING.

2008 THE OBAMA YEARS

Barry Soetoro, born 1961, attended Columbia University in the City of New York in 1981. The world knows him as Barack Obama.

Obama appears and takes the helm, and orchestrates the Arab Spring uprising. 311 is a Gematria number used by the Satanic Cult.

Obama has been resident in the basement of the White House, whilst Biden has been the pretend President, or Resident. Naturally, Biden has been obeying instructions.

SUN SUI ART OF WAR

Faith tells me that no matter what lies ahead of me, my angels are already there.

The US Generals investigation commenced in 1963, and considerable intelligence is being collected.

Obama has no problems as Hillary Clinton was right behind to complete his aims.

1 DEMORALISATION – PERIOD REQUIRED 15 TO 20 YEARS.

Truth will set you free – cannot allow that.
Freedom of speech – cannot allow that.
Dehumanise the deplorables, divide and conquer.
Deceive, distract, destroy nationalism, and patriotism.

A lot was achieved under Bush senior, Clinton, and Bush junior
Operation Paperclip introduced high ranking Nazis into America post-World War 11. George Bush Senior's father was a high ranking Nazi in an influential position who established the Nazi Post War Agenda, the Fourth Reich is alive and well.

Psychological warfare, high on the agenda MK Ultra mind control. Brainwash and subversion of the population worldwide.

Establish influencing bodies to control the thinking.
Control propaganda and information.
Control main stream media, and social media.
Create false narrative.

Insert key people to promote the plan worldwide.
Corrupt security agencies worldwide.
Corrupt all elections, control result worldwide.
Corrupt senate, congress representatives, lobbyists, and civil servants.
Corrupt Supreme Court Judges.
Corrupt state senators, judges, sheriffs, and local police.
Corrupt national police, lawyers, and state court judges.
Corrupt the military, air force, army, and navy forces.
Corrupt big pharma, big tech, military industrial complexes.
Corrupt non governing organisations.
Corrupt bankers, financiers, entrepreneurs.
Corrupt doctors, medical profession, and professors.

Corrupt college, and university professors and teachers.
Corrupt school teachers, parent teacher committees.
Corrupt teaching syllabus to students, LBGTQ+
Corrupt unions.
Corrupt farming and food industry.
Corrupt Hollywood.
Hollywood has produced films and documentaries over many years to project the satanic message to humanity. False Satanic doctrine has been implanted in our minds. Hugh Hefner of Playboy fame was financed by the CIA. LGBTQ+ ideas promote inhuman values against GOD and man, intended to split society and promote division.

Arm police, state guard, National Guard reserve, and state defence forces with military grade weapons.

Amend the laws, add new controlling laws, and emergency laws.

Remove weapons in private hands, disarm population.

Build 800 FEMA (Federal Emergency Management Agency) Concentration camps. Walmart stores adapted to become concentration camps. Build 800 guillotines.

Build nuclear shelters deep underground military bases. Provide D.U.M.B.s with food stocks for 150 years.

Pat Price was a CIA operative who remote viewed what was against the interests of the USA. He remote viewed alien deep underground military bases in Australia, Rhodesia (now Zimbabwe) Alaska and in an Indian Reservation in the USA, and established that many more existed. Unfortunately Pat Price was unaware that these fell under the control of the CIA, and he was poisoned in his hotel before he could identify more.

Build bio labs in foreign lands, 367 worldwide, with 46 of them in Ukraine alone. The reason for Russia's invasion is to destroy these laboratories.

Experiment and develop viruses and manufacture to scale, and also manufacture adrenachrome, opioids, and other drugs to scale, and distribute illegally throughout society.

Create false flag events to divert attention for media. Train sleepers to await mobilization for false flags. Train brainwashed individuals to carry out false flag events. Train brainwashed groups to carry out false flags. Train Antifa, BLM in the art of disguise to carry out rioting and looting. Blame the peaceful MAGA crowd.

Transfer crimes through disguise to opposition politicians.

Corrupt payments to supporters, sponsorships, bribes, blackmail of opposition and character assassination.

2 – DESTABILISATION – PERIOD REQUIRED 2 TO 5 YEARS.

News is trauma based mind control. Media coverage maximized against established authorities. Develop information and digital war against deplorables.

Police defunded.
Military defence defunded.

Create fear in the population. Pandemic introduced to activate emergency laws. Jet streaming of the virus to maximise exposure to the people. Compulsory vaccination introduced to destroy health. Hospitalisation to further destroy health.

Prevent transmissions by imposing control lockdowns. Extend lockdowns to escalate fear and control. Introduce compulsory masks to escalate control. Further controlled deterioration in human health.

Church not essential shut down, harass and close down.
GOD is not to interfere with Satan's plans.

Supreme Court legislated on abortion in 1973, against life.
Medical profession crush the heads of aborted babies. Profit by selling the foetuses for research?
Satan won a victory for death.
GOD wins a victory in 2022: Roe versus Wade overturned,
Scotus in GOD's hands at that moment in time.

Attack Congress blame the Opposition. Attack economy, collapse currency, escalate interest rates. Attack schools to create opportunities for disarming the population. Attack fuel supplies to destroy transport network. Attack Supreme Court for Roe versus Wade repeal. Attack shops, shoplifting becomes a pastime.

Create “global warming” weather events by manipulating it. Fires, flooding, hurricanes, storms, droughts, fog, tornadoes, earthquakes, volcanic eruptions, and space weather events visible around the globe.

Direct energy weapons, (DEW) start fires.
Cloud seeding and ion emitters control clouds, rain, and droughts.
HAARP weather warfare machines, high frequency radar installations worldwide.

“Rods from God” (false name) 20 x 1 foot hypersonic missiles, tectonic weapons used to attack underground tunnels, activate earthquakes, and volcanoes.

The explosion in Beirut I believe was one such event by man, which totally destroyed the economy of Lebanon. Beirut is a main centre for human trafficking.

Another event controlled by man was the Fukushima tsunami. The Japanese government was threatened allegedly by Netanyahu (false) with a nuclear undersea explosion, unless they paid a US$50 billion bribe, or doom.

DARPA: Defence Advanced Research Projects Agency – Who funds them? They developed Microsoft, Google, Google Maps, The Worldwide Web, Facebook, Twitter and much more.

EPA – Environmental Protection Agency was set up by Presidential Decree on February 11th, 1994, by Bill Clinton, and is NOT Constitutional.

The current situation is Scotus have a legal case pending to overturn this Presidential Decree, as the full Congress and Senate have to pass any and all environmental laws.
This means that all laws passed by EPA are invalid.

Foreign relations – start wars.
Pay for wars. Supply war materials to impoverish country.

Launder money by “paying” for wars.

Sleepers activated for nefarious false flag duties. Assassinating Japanese Shinzo Abe, ex PM is a false flag event. Brainwashed individuals and groups carry out false flags events. Antifa, BLM in disguise rioting and looting transferring blame for crimes on to opposition political supporters.

Rioters and looters act without legal action being taken against them. Civil war was promoted amongst the population.

Habeas Corpus act suspended, arrest, imprison without trial on innocent. Ken and Barbie Cromar versus IRS trial has been ongoing for five years. Corrupt law fare at work.

Emergency powers were used against peaceful protestors. January 6th, 2020 false flag event, arrested, still in jail no charges, no trial, no bail. Assets seized, confiscated, and sold without legal authority. Bank accounts are frozen.

Corrupt government approve and finance unrestricted illegal immigration. Over 3 million immigrants arrived in 2022 alone. Co-operate with foreign cartels for illegal activities. Co-operate with local mafia cartels for illegal activities.

Presidential decrees to promote green new deal objectives. Attack food supplies to create shortages. 10,000 beef cattle died mysteriously in Texas so far. Sabotage and derail coal trains to disrupt commerce. Restrict vehicles by legal means. Laws in California have forced 70,000 trucks off the road.
Chicken flu is introduced, commercial farms flocks destroyed in their millions. The turkey industry has been similarly decimated.
Food manufacturing outlets were attacked, over 102 closed down to date. Condemn baby food and milk manufacturing outlets shut down supply. F.D.A condemn EU baby food which is to a higher standard. F.D.A. approve poisonous foods.

3 – CRISIS STAGE: WE ARE IN THE STAGE 3 CRISIS.

CRY FOR A SAVIOUR – "COME BACK DONALD, ALL IS FORGIVEN"
Economy is destroyed, rioters and looters are taking control. Fear is high, insecurity is increasing. Food supplies short, empty shelves in shops.

Truckers cannot afford fuel, supplies delivery breaks down. Truckers delivering food attacked. Sleepers trained are activated to take over. Military activated. Bio currency, and identity chip in your hand to obtain food. A good time for the Biden's Chinese masters sleepers to move in.

Antichrist, Nazis, Fascists, Marxism, and Communism take over the reins of power.

4 – NORMALISATION: THE WORLD COUP STILL HAS TO REVEAL ITSELF.

The Department of Defence Law of War was activated on 6th November 2022 for the Mid Term Elections.

Is this the actions of the white hats or the black hats?

Overthrow the Government of the Day. Military authority takes over control of the country, whosoever controls the guns controls the day.
Rioters disappear, services no longer required, except as enforcers.

New normal, military takeover, fear rules, 1984 rules.

Resistance against a well-trained armed services difficult.

We have GOD, Jesus Christ his son, and the Holy Spirit on our side. How can we lose?

GAME OVER? WELL, NOT QUITE.

The American Democratic Party has two wings, one is weird, and the other is insane. The Republican Party has been corrupted by the hidden agenda of Satan.

The 2022 election results mean the Democrats control the Senate, and the Republicans control the House, with Kamala Harris, the Vice President, having a final vote on any issue put to the vote.

The above picture of the Art of War in the USA applies equally around the world. The difference is in the state of stability within these countries. Many manifest war, uprising, discontent, and instability.

The people of Sri Lanka rebelled against their government, truckers in Canada, farmers in the Netherlands followed by other EU countries are staging major protests leading to violent actions being taken by their respective governments.

On GOD's side are the well trained armed services, misled and corrupted by their generals and leaders.

WHAT DOES ALL THIS MEAN TO YOU AND ME?

Angels have no philosophy but love.

GLOBAL CHAOS PLANNED BY NEW WORLD ORDER.

Through Governments not representing their voters but rather representing the self- interest of Oligarks, Industrial Companies, Big Tech, Big Pharma, Medical Industry, Education, Military, Police, corruption exists at every level of Society.
All governments worldwide corrupt.

GLOBAL VIRUS DECIMATES HUMANITY

Police state rules to control movement of population.
Compulsory mandates force vaccination regime.
Compulsory masks introduced to interfere with breathing.
Concentration camp lockdowns restricting the movement of the population.
Huge unexplained deaths, 84% increase in males taking mRNA vaccine.

GLOBAL POLITICAL CHAOS.

Politicians are being manipulated by their civil servants, big tech, and all the global companies are paying bribes, blackmailing, and threatened. Pressure groups control the agenda.
Intent to destroy the financial security of the middle class in society. All weak characters attracted by free money.

GLOBAL TRADE AND TRANSPORT CHAOS

World trade falls off a cliff.
Shortage of foods, shortage of goods, shortage of fuels, increases prices of that available.
Lack of demand causes collapse of airlines, shipping industry, railway networks, trucking industry.
Industrial demand being down leads to increased unemployment.
Haulage prices explode.
In America, it is estimated that only 23 days of diesel fuel remained at time of election in 2022.

GLOBAL ENERGY CRISIS

Coal power stations closed,
Gas power stations closed,
Oil power stations closed,
Nuclear power stations closed.

GLOBAL FARMING CHAOS

Fuel, fertilizer, and seed costs explode, amidst shortages.
Food grown diminishes dramatically, famine is inevitable.

GLOBAL STOCKMARKET CHAOS

Stocks and shares value collapses. Many companies go bankrupt, severely contract production.

GLOBAL ECONOMIC CHAOS

Currency value collapses, inflating the cost of all goods.

Central and commercial banks declare bankruptcy.

Currency is paper, gold and silver are unobtainable.

How do you buy a loaf of bread with a gold bar?

GLOBAL SPIRITUAL AND MORAL CHAOS

Governments close down churches to stop the virus spread and dissent.

GLOBAL FAMILY CHAOS

Affected by side effects of virus, long COVID, vaccines, and Lock-down.

Bankrupted by falling incomes, rising mortgage, heating, fuel, and food costs.

GLOBAL COMMUNICATION CHAOS

All sources of information under one central control.

Newspapers, television, radio, and internet are controlled by fact checkers. The film industry is producing false narratives.

GLOBAL MILITARY CHAOS

Marshall Law introduced to maintain peace at a time of civil disturbance. Hopefully the powers of peace are in control, not the negative force of a dictatorship.

FOREIGN WARS

KOREA: 1950 – 1953 fight against communism.
VIETNAM: 1955 – 1975 fight against communism.
PANAMA: 1989 – 1990 Deposed leader Manual Noriega for drug trafficking. CIA has exclusive rights to drug trafficking.
BOSNIA: 1990 – 1995 Fight for freedom after break-up of Yugoslavia
IRAQ: 1990 – 1991 Kuwait invasion, weapons of mass destruction false, oil grab.
SOMALIA: 1992 Civil war.
AFGHANISTAN: 2001 – 2021 Cocaine poppy centre, money laundering, trafficking, CIA has exclusive rights to drug trafficking. Mineral rich country.
IRAQ: 2003 – 2011 Saddam Hussain wanted to go to gold standard. Oil grab. Half a million children died during the Iraq war.
LIBYA: 2011 Gadaffi wanted to go to a gold standard. Oil grab.

UKRAINE: 2021 - ? Money laundering, opium, fentanyl, adrenachrome, organ smuggling, human and child trafficking. Keep World Economic Forum business interests secret.

WORLD NUCLEAR WAR SCARE? – WORLD WAR 111 which involves the COSMOS.

Many options in the hands of the World Economic Forum and Alien A.I. pulling the strings of power.

Taiwan v China, North v South Korea, Iran v Israel, USA/Ukraine v Russia, USA v China
The Evergreen ship which blocked the Suez Canal was believed to be carrying arms, including nuclear weapons to start a war in the Middle East.

06 October, 2022, USA Special Forces are in Ukraine.

UN/NATO/ILLUMINATTI/USA Special Forces at war with Russia in Ukraine. Al Qaeda and Isis fighters being paid by Ukraine, NATO, USA to fight for Ukraine against Russia.

The only country to benefit from the sabotage of Russia's Nordstream 1 and 2 natural gas pipelines is America, who are now selling fracking gas to Europe and the UK at 500% increase in price.

It is claimed that UK Forces sabotaged the Nordstream Gas Pipelines and the Crimean Bridge. Liz Truss phoned Blinken to say “It is done.” This could also mean that she had a normal bowel movement!

Payment by the New World Order normally happens after Politicians leave their positions as Prime Movers of Government Policy approved by the World Economic Forum. How did Mr Tony Blair get so rich so quickly?

HOW DOES GOD FIGHT BACK?

HOW DOES GOD, AND THE WHITE HATS FIGHT AGAINST THIS INFESTATION, AND VIOLENT ACTIONS ON THE PART OF AN EVIL MANKIND?

Sometimes angels sing to you in the wind.
All you have to do is listen.

Acting without the enemy knowing. Lots of lying and propaganda confuses the enemy too. Many enemy leaders and lead followers have been removed.

Cloning has been carried out by man and of man since the 1930s, if not before. Mankind only found out when Dolly the sheep was introduced to the world.

These substitutes, and those of the enemy who have been turned are providing valuable information, and carrying out instructions to benefit the white hats.

A covert war has been ongoing for the last 70 years since 1952, but only recognised in 1963 by the White Hats after the death of John F Kennedy.

The Processional Astronomical Clock, predicts the Electro Magnetic Pulse from the sun will strike earth by 2024, as described elsewhere. This flash will take down the Beast, the evil A.I. that is on the earth.

Our DNA is going to be re-activated to 4d and 5d. Aging will stop. A Quantum Shift of Evolution will take place.

Organised religion is coming to an end, it is a doctrine introduced, and sadly has been manipulated by man.

GOD will arise above religious hierarchy, man should learn to meditate to GOD 30 minutes a day, and Pray.

GREAT GLOBAL WARMING HOAX

HOW DOES THE EARTH FUNCTION?

Feathers appear when angels are near.

Plato, who lived from 427 BCE to 347 BCE, suggested a 5,000 to 6,000 year cycle of disaster. The earth's elliptical plane with extreme tilt suggested a strong gravitational pull causing disruption, cause unknown, object in space?

We are currently undergoing a war on earth, and in the heavens, and man is not responsible.

The Great Global Warming Hoax Being Caused by Man is Unproven Theories, which are sensationalised and repetitively repeated in the Main Stream Media by voices representing the misdirected World Economic Forum Political and Economic Agenda, so that we do not forget.

THE EARTH

The earth spins at roughly 1,000 miles per hour on its magnetic axis. It does a complete rotation of the earth in approximately 24 hours, one earth day.

It is in effect with all the electrical stored energy a dynamo which man has not yet learned to harness.

All this stored atmospheric energy is expressed in the storm systems which regularly attack the earth releasing that energy on to the earth's surface.

The earth revolves around the sun at 67,000 miles per hour. It takes approximately 1 year, (365+ days) to go around the sun.

The Great Pyramid of Giza, in ratio to the earth is 1/43,200 to the earth. This number repeats (432 Hz)

EARTH'S GEOMETRIC LEY LINES

The earth is covered in what would appear to be random lines of invisible positive energy. These must cover millions of miles over land and sea.

These have been recognised by ancient civilisations, but modern man has not studied, or understood their true importance. Ancient civilisations constructions are centred round these meeting/crossing points, and end points of these Ley lines. These were recognised as special spiritual places using marking, or standing stones.

Stonehenge in Wiltshire, Calanais on the Isle of Lewis, are well known examples of them in the United Kingdom.

Mark stones and Standing stones exist, which suggests that perhaps, the Ley lines were used to identify the sun and star systems in the sky for navigation over land and water purposes. These ley lines pre date Christianity, and there original function is lost to prehistoric and modern man.

The Ley lines in the UK cover the length and breadth of the UK, and are 21 in number, and cover

3,604 miles in their accumulated length. This is probably an understatement of the total UK Ley lines.

What of the rest of the world?

How did man discover these Ley lines?

Perhaps in pre-historic times, our space alien ancestors used these ley lines as anti-gravity railway tracks. They followed the natural earth force to their destination. Man stranded on earth was being transported around, as the Navvies or labourers of the day, and the knowledge was handed down.

EARTH'S MAGNETIC FIELD DECLINATION AND STRENGTH

The movement of the earth's magnetic field is caused by the movement of the earth's magnetic core.
Movement of the magnetosphere of our planet magnetically north/south balance maintains protection for the earth from the solar system. Solar winds will attack the earth and create

extreme weather events, storms hurricanes, tsunamis, earthquakes, and volcanic action.

Magnetic field varies through time, and has been a matter of record since 1590 AD, until today, waxing and waning, currently at its weakest. Weather events will therefore be much more extreme at this time 2022 AD.

Jet streams are increasing in power but this is due to the earths weakening magnetic field, and direction.

The earth's magnetic field declination varies from 30 degrees west at the southern tip of Africa, to 26 degrees east at the tip of New Zealand.

Does the above affect the earth's weather? Rain, ice, snow, storms, lightning? Absolutely yes, and man has no control.

EARTH'S MAGNETIC DIRECTION

This is monitored historically through analysis of magnetic magma in volcanic eruption. Activity traps the earth's magnetic field in the lava at that moment in time.

The location of magnetic North changes at about 35 miles per year towards Siberia. In 75 years, it has travelled about 2,625 miles eastward. Your grandad's compass is out of date.
Does this affect the earth's weather? Rain, ice, snow, storms, lightning?

The ice at the South Pole is reported to be melting – true, but what is not reported is the ice is increasing in other areas of the South Pole.

Antarctic in the west is melting, and in the east the ice is growing. The amount of ice melt in the west is estimated to be 82 million tonnes. The west of Antarctic has volcanoes, and as in the rest of the world volcanic activity is ongoing, heating the land and melting the ice.

Absolutely yes, and man is not responsible.

REVERSAL OF POLES

This has been recorded through the above volcanic activity, and has happened five times through dating the rock. These were extinction events with the earth's magnetic field effectively turned off and upside down.

The magnetism would form patterns like a dog after it has a swim, and it shakes the water off its long hair. This would cause failure of the protection that the magnetic field provides.

These events cover a time period on earth of 78,000 years. The next will be the 6th. We could be at that time with the current location of the poles. That event will have a major impact on the human race. Refer further to the earth's precession astronomical clock.

The Aliens – Pleaidians have installed on Antarctic the TESLA SCALAR TECHNOLOGY to correct the earth's magnetic direction and prevent the earth flipping. This has taken 10 years to construct, and will strengthen the earth's magnetic field. Tesla technology has been operating since 2012 AD, counteracts the earth out of place magnetic field. This is an artificial magnetic field to strengthen the earth's field.

Anyone interested in what happens to the planet when the poles reverse – research EDGAR CAYCE, the sleeping prophet's prophecy.

ANTARTIC CONVERGENCE

The Southern Ocean is the body of very cold water that surrounds Antarctica, and spins in sympathy with the earths spinning. This body of cold water meets the warmer water of the Atlantic, Indian, and Pacific Oceans at the convergence, which is also spinning with the earth. This cold/hot barrier insulates Antarctica from the Northern warm water.
Polar Vortex winds are increasing making the air colder.

THE EARTH'S "WOBBLE" OR PRECESSION OF THE EQUINOXES.

The earth's axis is tilted at 23.5 degrees relative to its plane of motion around the sun. The earth "wobbles" around the sun over a period of time. Calculated from the Great Pyramid of Giza, this period is 25,826.5 years.

The Mayan precession astronomical clock is 25,920 years. This clock expired on 21st December 2012, and started anew the next day. This before man invented the compass?
Wikipedia is accurate to 26,000 years, but the origin of this is unknown. Currently to the writer's knowledge, it is not precisely determined by modern scientists.

WHAT IS THE PRECESSION ASTRONOMICAL CLOCK?

The earth travels around the sun trapped in a beneficial orbit with minor variations. The sun travels around the galaxy at 135 miles per second. It will not return to this moment in time and place for 25,826.5 earth years.
It could be said that this period of time is one sun year.

Solar storms, sun spots, and flares affect the earth and currently the sun is undergoing an increased activity which is expected to end soon, but not yet.

The solar cycles have been monitored since 1755, we are now in the 25th cycle. The new cycle started in 2019, and we are entering solar flare Maximus. The cycle is approximately 11 years, but there is a magnetic cycle of 22 years. The Maximus sun flare cycle is seven years, started and will peak around July 2025.

The sun, like the moon, waxes and wanes.

There is a planet "X" beyond Pluto, orbiting a dead star, 50 billion miles away from the sun which orbits near the earth and sun every 13,000 years.

The sun is at its closest proximity to the "black" sun, dead or "death" star. Both our sun and the dead star have strong gravitational influences on each other, and on earth. This results in an increase in the sun's solar storms, sun spots and flares which are currently frequent.

Heat build-up in the sun is due to the near proximity of the dead star. Cold build up in the sun is due to its extreme distance from the dead star.

The dark sun, with its increased gravitational pull on the sun and earth is a death star to earths inhabitants experienced in the past five extinction events. It has a 1000 times greater gravitational pull than earth's sun. This star is super dense and 4 to 5 times the size of earth. It was identified at 50 billion miles distant. It is now 4.7 billion miles away.

This close to earth, the earth is reacting to a major increase in movements in the earth's plates. Earthquakes and volcanoes on land and below the seas are causing disruption, and perhaps expansion of the earth.

The result is the earth is giving up its stored heat, causing warming of the planet, on land and in the oceans in the areas of activity.

Scientists were puzzled by the deviation evident on all planets in the cosmos. What universal force was influencing these planets orbits and deviation?

The USA Pioneer 10 satellite launched in 1972 was sent to Planet Jupiter. The Pioneer 11 satellite launched in 1973 was sent in the opposite direction. The signals they both sent back determined the existence of the dark sun, or dead star. Equal gravitational pull was identified by both Pioneer 10 and 11, showing the presence of a dead star affecting the whole solar system.

The two scientists who interpreted the information from these satellites were Robert Harrington, head of the US Navy Observatory, and Thomas van Flander, who was the astronomer with the correct answer to the puzzle.

At that point, information was announced by NASA, and then withdrawn and covered up by NASA. The individuals were ridiculed and denounced. Sound familiar?

Both these men mysteriously died very soon after their solution was released. Their answer was ridiculed and the information removed from the media. Further research by others exposed the lies by the authorities.

The effect this knowledge had probably caused mass panic among the elites, governments, illuminati, and deep state operatives of the day, and continues to haunt them.

The above would be very motivational to secretly build around the world deep underground military bases, to enable the elites and their servants to hide underground prior to the great solar flash striking the earth.

It is a logical explanation on the drought conditions being encountered in the major rivers and dams around the world.
The drought conditions affecting the major world's rivers has been prophesied in the Bible, God is never wrong, he knows what is past, and what is to come.

The whisky industry in Scotland is not affected at this time.

All ancient knowledge is being hidden so that our civilisation does not find out what happened with great regularity in every past 13,000 years.

The solar flares hitting the earth at this time are stimulating the human 3 dimensional physical and spiritual attributes. These flares enhance the physical and spiritual attributes to a 4th dimensional astral state. This changes the body from a carbon state to a crystalline state.
God is providing the human race with a spiritual upgrade.
Those that have had the mRNA vaccines are disabled from having the update.
Human dormant DNA is activated by the great solar flash, (EMP) electromagnetic pulse.
Every 13,000 years, in accordance with the astronomical clock, there is an explosive event. This is due about now, and will be a great solar flash. Rainbow clouds will appear in the sky at the time of the flash.

It is difficult to be accurate, but predictions estimate by May 2023, or May 2024.

Will this cause a catastrophic melt of the Antarctica ice?

Noah and the Ark come to mind. God states that there will be no more floods on the scale of Noah's flood.

Dr Murray Cook, Stirling Council Archaeologist has done a study of Scottish Prehistoric Hill Forts which all show signs of extreme heat melting the rocks. Is the great solar flash the explanation?

The Mayans prophesied that there would be five extinction events, and the sixth would not take place, nobody would be harmed and the planet would be blessed with "rainbow children."

Humanity will transfer to the 5th dimension, instead of a 2 strand DNA, 3rd dimension, it will grow to a four and five strand DNA, 4 and 5 dimension.

The above DNA enhancement will be further increased with the solar flash. The good news is the solar flash destroys the destructive toxins which are present in the body, with the mRNA vaccines. Graphene is a liquid metal that interferes with the bodies "electrical wiring."

The beating heart is regulated by electrical pulses, interfere with that, using graphene, and the heart is the first to be impacted.

Hopefully, this will totally negate the mRNA vaccine implanted in the body worldwide. A big wormhole now with more people dying post COVID-19 than from the virus.

The solar flash will activate the pineal gland, which receives vibrational frequencies. It is suggested the solar flash will be an ascension event as described in the bible.

The earth, too, will change its vibrational frequency to 44Hz on the great solar flash.

There is a down-side; the great solar flash which is coming is an electromagnetic pulse.
Electrical devices will have to be disconnected from the National Grid. Satellites, electric cars, mobile phones, phones, televisions, and computers, are likely to turn into redundant electronics. They will all have to be protected.

Prophets have prophesied many stars and meteors will cross the sky over the next period, observed over Grangemouth/Glasgow in Scotland 14th September 2022.

THE SUN

The electromagnetic charge from the sun causes opposite poles and superheating of the sun and earth. The current earth's magnetic field is 1000's of miles off course.
The dark star is 1000 times more powerful than the earth's sun.

In 1859, a major solar sun storm struck earth, known as the Carrington Event. It was the biggest solar flare to strike earth in recorded history. It was seen in the night sky over three nights.

Diameter of sun = 864,000 miles
Diameter of sun = 108 times diameter of earth
Distance between earth and sun = 864,000 miles x 108 = 93,000,000 miles
Earth to sun alternatively is = 149,597,887 km

108 is a Holy Number.

THE MOON

The diameter of the moon is 1,080 miles, roughly John O Groats to Land's End. It travels around the earth at 2,288 miles per hour, and orbits the earth in 27.3 days, but 29.5 days to change from old moon to new moon.
The moon moves 12 – 13 degrees east every day. The moonrise is, therefore, delayed about 50 minutes every day.

The earth's axis toward the sun is controlled by the dark star and the moon. NASA states the moon is also affected by the dark star. The moon syncronistically rotates around the earth, so we never see the back of the moon.

A lunar eclipse happened on 8th November 2022, a blood moon. A lunar eclipse is also expected on 28th October, 2023. On December 21st, 2022, New Moon, the Age of Aquarius began.

The manned Apollo moon landing on the 20th July, 1969, took many photographs of the moon from the front that we can see from earth, and the back of the moon, which cannot be seen from earth. All

Apollo and other lunar trips were similarly recorded with photographs.

Lt Col Johnson was involved at that time, and was responsible for indexing and analysing these photographs, which were made in several copies of first generation photos. These photographs proved, without a shadow of doubt, that the moon contained Alien moon bases, from ancient, and modern times. These photos were kept as one set, with negatives, but Lt Johnson kept a set, and all others were destroyed. Many years later, these photos were recovered and all with alien structures were adjusted to delete all traces from the record.

The USA Government or Deep State wish to obliterate the record from history.

It is thought that man has secretly returned to the moon, in co-operation with the big Tech Corporations, Deep State and Aliens, they have a manned base.

There are many who can prove that the moon acts as an alien space station. Good alien or bad, I cannot tell. USA public moon landings set up sound and vibration devices to transmit, and after the landers returned the astronauts to their earth return vehicle, the landers were dropped on to the moon. This resulted in a sound of a bell ringing for several days, suggesting the moon is indeed hollow.

The Zulu Nation with no written language, has a verbal tradition handing down the ancient beginnings of the earth, and sky. Their Medicine Men recounting the story that a sky people brought the moon to the earth at a later time after the earth was formed. This is supported by other tribal communities, the American Indians have a rich history of tribal folklore.

The effect of the moon on earth and the oceans is greater than the effect of man. The tides and winds are directly affected by the waxing and waning of the moon. The storms and weather are also affected.

It is suggested that a woman's menstruation is controlled by the moon.

The full effects of the moon on land are not so clear. I believe it has an effect on earthquake and volcanic eruptions.

The Moon's position in the galaxy, exactly blocks out the sun in a solar eclipse.

Earth to moon: 384,403 kms
Earth to sun: 149,597,887kms
Diameter of sun = 108 times diameter of earth

THE VAN ALLEN RADIATION BELT: PROTECTING EARTH FROM EXTERNAL FORCES.

Zone of energetic charged particles most of which originate from solar wind. They are captured and held around our planet by the planet magnetosphere.

Earth has two such belts, and sometimes others are temporarily created.

I see the hand of GOD in such a creation to protect earth.

The two belts extend from an altitude of about 640 km, to 58,000 km above the surface of the earth in which regional radiation levels vary. Most particles are solar wind, the magnetic field deflects those energetic particles and protects the atmosphere from destruction.

There is an inner and outer radiation belt. The belt endangers satellites, which must be protected in vulnerable areas.

These belts would be severely affected by the earth's polar reversal.

I HAVE DESCRIBED HOW THE EARTH FUNCTIONS BUT NOT

WHAT DESTRUCTIVE MAN IS UP TO

Bill Clinton introduced the Environmental Protection Agency by Decree.

This is unconstitutional, introduced illegal laws promoting the hoax. Climate change is a constructed narrative.

New World Order defines the argument construct, and counter argument.

New World Order form propaganda movements (EPA) to destroy opposition.

Vice President Al Gore was a candidate for USA President in 2000, but lost to George Bush Junior. He was rewarded with promotion within the World Economic Forum to head up the Global Warming Hoax Cast of Theatrics.

Gain a new income stream through the introduction of "GREEN TAXES", introduced to "green" the environment.

Greta Thunberg is not an innocent who is consciously promoting an obsession with doom.

She is allegedly a Rothschild. She is well trained, and groomed by her manipulators.

No acknowledgement of Antarctica ice fields wax and wane annually.
No acknowledgement of effect of moving magnetic field.
No acknowledgement of effect of earth's wobble.
No acknowledgement of moon's activity effect on climate over time.
No acknowledgement of sun's activity over time waxing and waning.
No acknowledgement of sun spot activity effect on climate over time.
No acknowledgement of dark star in the cosmos, effect on climate over time.

The above has been touched on to show how the earth functions.

In defence of the climate warriors, much needs to be done by man to clean up his environment of pollutants that man has introduced by his activities.

Industry needs to be held to a higher standard and made responsible worldwide for their negligence.

Industries need to be charged for pollution, which in the past has been ignored, providing ever inflated dividends to the elites. Methods of recycling have to be improved.

In dry climates, plastic containers could be used as planters limiting water use in drought environments.

Grow eco-friendly vegetables in arid and other climates limiting water use. Israel is far ahead in the cultivation of crops in an arid desert environment.

Africa already uses plastic cut up as aggregate to make concrete building blocks, where no stone aggregate is available.
The presence of micro plastic particles in Antarctica snow is a serious cause for concern, as it means man is absorbing these particles into his body around the world.

Why did Obama and Pelosi buy seaside beachfront summer properties?

Joe Biden owns a Caribbean Island.

Much effort has gone into using weather weapons to create a global warming effect around the world, which the new world order can exploit for political gain and mainstream media false flag publicity.

GLOBAL WEATHER EVENTS AND WEAPONS

1 ACTS of GOD – EVENTS

When angels visit us, we do not hear the rustle of their wings. We feel the love they create.

GOD always announces the news before the news through his prophets. These major weather events are, therefore, identifiable through prophecy.

The acts of GOD are clear today as they have been recent and extreme in nature, much more serious than man's abilities to manipulate weather.

Volcanic eruptions, earthquakes, storms, and tsunamis are happening around the world. The earth's plates "ring of fire" is very active.

There has been an earthquake swarm in Lake Talpo, New Zealand, site of super volcano where there were over 700 tremors up to 4.4 on the Richter Scale. There was an undersea Caldera quake between north and south island.

A prophecy made and repeated is GOD will destroy Washington DC by storms, but will ensure that the Lincoln Memorial remains untouched.

The main reason for the acts of GOD extreme weather at the moment is to stop wars starting between countries and men, because the economy and men are overwhelmed by extreme weather events, making war difficult. It hopefully will also stop civil wars, as man seeks to help his fellow man. Also, with the prophecies it wakens man up to GOD.

GOD has already caused 1,000 tremors at Yellowstone and the Park is closed to the general public.

GOD has the power to create a volcanic super eruption. The mountains surrounding Yellowstone will disappear after a super eruption takes place. The ash cloud rises and falls on at least 11 states, caused by the void of ash and magma being thrown into the air. The ash cloud around the world for several years would create a global volcanic winter.

If a super eruption takes place, six years of food supply is needed to overcome shortages worldwide caused by crop failure. Everything destroyed for hundreds of miles and around the world.

Global cooling after a VEI8 like Yellowstone super eruption, which is 1,000 times bigger than the Mount St Helen eruption. World temperatures drop 10% to 20% destroying 50% to 100% of life. This is in GOD's power. This would cause worldwide famine.

GOD has absolute control, therefore, GOD's weather events exceed mans. GOD has also prophesied a volcanic eruption in Sweden at a dormant volcano.

Many more prophecies are being made daily.

2 – ACTS OF MAN – SECRET WEATHER WARFARE

Believe in guardian angels. They believe in you and are always by your side.

All changes in the weather are blamed on human activities by the United Nations, a Cabal Organisation. This is, in my view, not true, the external influences on Earth are much more powerful than man's activities.

A contrail is a condensation flowing out of the engines of a jet. This is the by-product of jet engines.

A chem-trail is a sprayed desiccate particle trail from tanks within the plane anywhere worldwide, napalm and Agent Orange have been used in the past.

The chem-trail contents are heavily influenced by Bill Gates, one of the plans of the Cabal was to block out the sun, and prevent everyone's DNA uplift happening. This was done by the use of Nano

Aluminium and Barium Strontium Nano particles being released into the atmosphere.

It is called climate engineering, and promotes the one world climate agenda to introduce its green carbon tax agenda (or other) think Agent Orange which defoliated the jungle and introduced cancer to the Vietnamese population.

It is also targeted weather warfare introduced by spraying desiccate particles for two years. Then, start a forest fire because the forest has been sprayed with fire enhancing properties.

Cloud seeding is used to create rain, storms, hurricanes, tornadoes, floods, the opposite is drought.

It is an ideal medium for spreading virus's and forest fires around the earth. It is a weapon of power and control.

HAARP – HIGH FREQUENCY ACTIVE AURORAL RESEARCH PROGRAMME.

HAARP – Ionosphere Research Instrument (IRI) officially closed down in Alaska by USA in 2014, but now more than 100 built around the world.

High powered high frequency phased array radio transmitter with a set of 180 antennas, disposed in an array of 12 x 15 units that occupy a rectangle of about 30 to 40 acres. It creates electromagnetic waves which heats up the atmosphere.
It is an ionosphere heater – 3.5 million watts of power. Heat creates rotations, and the outcome is storms, hurricanes, tornadoes, the opposite is drought.

It creates deluges, and the opposite is droughts around the world. It is a weapon of power and control.

DIRECT ENERGY WEAPONS.

These are satellites which can direct Laser Energy Beams to areas of forest to start fires.

This is used to burn national forest reserves to permit the harvesting of timber after a fire, which would otherwise be protected. It is a weapon of power and control with commercial benefit.

"RODS FROM GOD" (MISNAMED)

20 X 1 Foot hypersonic missiles. These are fired from space, and activating earthquakes and volcanoes. Invented by Nicola Tesla many years ago, they are very accurate.

Space Force explosive kinetic energy weapons. They are being used to destroy the underground maglev train tunnels at 6,000 to 10,000 feet below ground level covering the earth.

ATOMIC WEAPONS.

These create undersea tsunamis, earthquakes to overwhelm coastlines. An example of this is the Japanese coast and Fukushima nuclear power station being overwhelmed. They are easily transported by submarine, and can shut down a nuclear power source for mankind.

Man can imitate GOD by exploding a nuclear device in Yellowstone Park. There are rumours that nuclear devices have been implanted in Cambridge, London, Paris, Berlin and Warsaw, and other places around Europe with the intention to blame Russia. Fear and panic are weapons, it does not make sense for mankind to start a nuclear war, and destroy earth.

Tectonic weapons are used to attack the underground tunnels.

FERTILIZER

This created the biggest non-nuclear man-made explosion in history in Beirut, Lebanon. This totally destroyed the economy of Lebanon. Beirut is a main centre for human trafficking.

DARPA – DEFENCE ADVANCED RESEARCH PROJECTS AGENCY.

A branch of the Department of Defence. Developed Microsoft, Google, Google Maps, Facebook, Twitter, and controls the internet, the World Wide Web.

Darpa is a corrupt AI which operates independently on behalf of the World Economic Forum.
COVID-19 is a military grade weapon shielded by Pfizer, and Moderna. Potomac Research Group work on Darpa Adapt: Protect Programme Platform planned in 2012 against pandemic. Growing the virus, and ending the virus in 60 days with the vaccine. Gene encoded vaccines developed by Moderna and Pfizer.
Moderna/Fauci own the patent on the Moderna vaccine.
Moderna claimed a vaccine 3 days after COVID-19 Emergency was declared. Moderna is suing Pfizer for patent infringement.
Refer further to NIH – National Institute of Health a medical research agency.

Anthony Fauci, Chief Medical Advisor to the President of USA Inc. He was involved in the creation of HIV, Aids epidemic and also in the creation of COVID-19.
The origin of COVID-19 is thought to be from an off-world Alien species.

Fauci withheld medicines for COVID-19 that worked.

He created a dangerous vaccine. False testing by manipulating test to obtain false results.

Authorised and instructed the carrying out of sadistic experiments on animals and humans.

Dr Kary Mullis spent 30 years trying to expose Dr Fauci. A serial killer, is he of the Joseph Mengele bloodline?

Christine Grady, is head of “NIH Bio Ethics” a company that approves the Drugs for the FDA, and is also married to Anthony Fauci.
AIDS – US Patent 5676977
H1N1 – US Patent 8835624
EBOLA – US Patent 20120251502
SWINE FLU – US Patent CA2741523 A1

BSE – US Patent 0070031450 A1
ZIKA – ATTC VR – 84 ROCKEFELLER FOUNDATION
SARS – US Patent 7897744 and 8506968
CORONAVIRUS – US Patent 10130701
Biometric tests for Covid 19 – US Patent 20200279585 A1 Proof that Richard A Rothschild knew in 2015, and 2017.
Scheduled Publication date 3rd September 2020.

They knew in 2015 what was going to happen by September 2020. First registration: Netherlands, October 15, 2015. You were never sick, you were poisoned.

The toxic ingredients in your children's vitamins.
Vitamin B12 – Cyanocobalamin is a derivation of cyanide and cobalt.

Ratheon and Lockhead Martin have a considerable number of patents for their secret military developments. The staff are all illegally controlled by non-disclosure agreements.

TR3b Black Mantra Salvatore Kaisi Patent Stealth Craft completely invisible. USA Military built it as an Anti-Gravity Spy Plane Patent Number US 1014453282.

There are hints that satellite technology now has the ability to x-ray the earth in great detail to the centre of the earth. How that is done is a mystery.

Darpa Budget 3.5 billion dollars in 2019.

CEDRON LARGE HADRON COLLIDER IN GENEVA SWITZERLAND, CIA HEADQUARTERS

This has been built below an ancient Temple of Apollo, with Shiva an ancient Goddess of Destruction, erected at the entrance. The W.H.O. met with China, and the Shiva Goddess of Destruction was at the head of the table.

A prophecy was made Air Force One would fly into the ground upside down. This was interpreted to mean that the USA would never have another President. The man behind Biden is Obama who poses as the Goddess Shiva. The Black Hats were attempting to open a portal at Cern for evil spirits.

Cedron Large Hadron Collider has now been recovered by the White Hats, to prevent Evil from flourishing.

RONALD REAGAN said that man is one generation away from losing everything.

The question must be asked – who are the influencers/manipulators? Who are the Pharaohs of today in these modern biblical times?

The power of prayer to our LORD GOD will overwhelm Satan.

WORLD UNDERGROUND CRIMINAL ORGANISATIONS

ILLUMINATI – NEW WORLD ORDER IS THE OFFICIAL WEBSITE - ANTICHRIST

PROMOTING ONE WORLD GOVERNMENT THROUGH WORLD ECONOMIC FORUM

Hollywood films used to promote the message, they want to protect mainstream and social media control of the propaganda message.
Trans Denominational Church control society through social division.
Music also used as a control medium.
Drugs, opium, fentanyl, and adrenachrome are used as a control medium.
Blackmail is used as a control medium.
MK Ultra mind control used to train destructive behaviour.
Assassination is used as instrument of eliminating dissent.

209 – 214 Countries corrupt governments and deep state operatives.
WORLD WIDE KEY PLAYERS INCLUDE:

HARAHI- Satan's false prophet, KLAUS SCHWAB, GEORGE SOROS, HENDRY KISSINGER, BARACK OBAMA, BILL GATES, MARK ZUCKERBERG, BRESINSKY, BIDEN, BILL and HILLARY CLINTON, GEORGE BUSH, TONY BLAIR, JUSTIN TRUDEAU, ROCKEFELLERS, ROTHSCHILDS, BILDERBERG GROUP, GUTTENBERG GROUP, TRILATERAL COMMISSION, KNIGHTS TEMPLAR, FREEMASON, JESUITS, DAVOS GROUP, ZALINSKY, QUEEN ELIZABETH 11, ROYALS of Belgium, Netherlands, Spain, Norway, VATICAN POPE, and many others around the world in strategic positions of power and influence.

The Forum of Young Global Leaders is educating hundreds of people annually, brainwashed and placed into positions of government and industrial power and influence to take over from their elders.

The governments of the world are currently controlled by corrupted elections, placing WEF sympathisers into power.
The level of corruption is extensive down to teachers, and parent teacher groups. The medical professions are now servants of big pharma, and their agenda of creating illness out of opportunity. First do no harm, is now last.

The Governments secret services, C.I.A., F.B.I., M.I.5., M.I.6., M.O.S.S.A.D., and many others around the world are utilised to expedite illegal government policy through direct methods, or employing criminals to carry out the criminality.

The USA Governments Federal Reserve Bank and 12 Central Banks are under the control of criminals and fraudsters.

The World Bank, I.M.F. B.I.S. are controlled by criminals and fraudsters.

The USA I.R.S. is a registered company in Haiti, and all the income tax is forwarded to the Vatican.

The W.H.O. is owned by Bill Gates, and the WEF desire is to place W.H.O. in charge of the world wide big pharma and the medical profession, who are now openly promoting in legislation around the world sickness and euthanasia.

The U.N. and NATO are controlled by the World Economic Forum their representatives promoting war, famine, sickness and euthanasia.
The mainstream media, Cinema, TV, Microsoft, Google, Apple, Facebook, are totally controlled by

WEF, and promotes WEF propaganda. Elon Musk in purchasing Twitter has raised the veil on a dark culture of crime at every level. More revelations are to come.

The Companies of the world currently controlled through three world wide companies, BLACKROCK, VALIANT and STATE STREET. Blackrock and Valiant hold shares in each other's company to create equilibrium.
They, in turn, hold collectively the majority of shares in the major worldwide companies, thus controlling industry actions and investments through a phone call.

Their illegal activities are covered up and hidden behind Lawfare to defend their actions.

The above organisations have access to the criminal families and minds worldwide so, Cosa Nostra, Italian Mafia, Kazarian Mafia, Australian Two Families, UK Six Families, Chinese, Japanese, and all countries criminal gangs have access to Government sponsored and approved criminality without consequences.
Balfour Agreement, Rothschild's Lease of the country of Israel has now expired. Israel will be

returned to Turkey, or perhaps to the United States of America. A clear line of action has not yet been revealed.

The American Government, and their deep state partners, avoid their FREEDOM OF INFORMATION ACTS by placing all their military programmes and projects with Private Corporations. The Government is protected from investigations. All reverse engineering of alien space ships and technology is carried out by private contractors.

A STRANGLEHOLD ON FINANCIAL CONTROLS.

The USA Government issues US $100 billion in Bonds borrowing instruments to the FED central bank. Costs? Paper costs cents.

FED lends US $100 billion in currency notes to the government and charge interest on the transaction, which are issued to the people.

The FED is then allowed to lend out US $900 billion in loans to the people and charge interest on the loans, covered by the value of the assets, which are used to borrow the money. If there was no

currency in debt, there would be no money in circulation. Perpetual debt is guaranteed.
The money to pay the interest does not exist.
A massive fraud prevails.

Only 10% of the funds are valid. 90% of funds in the FED are created out of nothing. This money is counterfeit and illegal.
It is further exaggerated by your local bank having US $100 million on deposit to create their own financial pyramid.

10,000 branches = 100 billion x 9 = US $900 billion to lend. How many in the USA?
75,000 branches = 900 billion x 7.5 = US $6,750 billion to lend.
Use of the US$ demonstrates what is going on worldwide in all the currencies. Fractional reserve lending policy is a system of modern slavery and doomed to failure.

How are these financial plans implemented internationally?

Economic hitmen are sent to bribe where required.
Jackals are sent to overthrow the governments.
Foreign military go to war where the jackal fails.

Corporacracy move to control politicians and become a politocracy. Democracy is dead. Vote meaningless.

The US Government Debt now exceeds US $31.4 trillion.
Congress must pass a new law to increase the debt burden on the taxpayers.
Republicans have just taken over responsibility. Why would they take on the Democratic Debt? They are controlled by a malignant unseen force.
US Treasury borrowing Authority has reached its debt ceiling. Catastrophic blow to the US Economy is coming.
Government Shutdown is highly probable.

Joe Biden asked Congress to pass his HR6666: US $6.5 billion Bio Research Bill to fund the World Economic Forum illegal activities.

Gavin Newsom, the Governor of California, has with his Committee for Reparations for Housing Discrimination against Descendants of Slaves, has awarded US $223,200 dollars to each, amounting to US $569 Billion Dollars bill for the taxpayers of California. The biggest taxpayer funded restitution in Californian History.

The Lunatics are in charge of the Asylum.

2016 - WHAT WENT WRONG?

DONALD J TRUMP with GOD's support wins the election, takes the helm of USA INC.
The Generals asked him to stand as a Presidential Candidate. The President and Commander in Chief was appointed on 20th January, 2017.

Fake news becomes the news. Truth becomes a casualty, but has actually been a casualty for a long time.

2016 – US REPUBLIC CAPITAL formed in RENO.
Gold from the Twin Towers recovered from the Vatican.

2017 – 20th May - Trump visited Saudi Arabia, Israel, Palestine Territories, Brussels, Vatican and Sicily.
Israel agreed to a Treaty with the Arab Countries.
Saudi Arabia appointed Donald Trump as King with the handover of the Royal Sword of Authority.
Vatican submitted to USA Terms of surrender demands.

2018 – 13th July – Trump visited the Queen at Buckingham Palace.

2019 – 3rd June – Donald Trump visited the Queen at Windsor Castle. The Queen and the Crown submit to the USA Terms of surrender demands.
Donald Trump became the owner of Australia, Canada and the USA.
2019 5th December, I believe the Queen died this day. Who then is acting the part? Is she an actor? Is she a clone? Is she a reptilian? Or was she making bramble jam/jelly? History will reveal the truth.
Donald Trump made America Great again and reduced unemployment. Made America energy independent, rebuilt the armed services. He created the Space Force and Starlink Satellite System. He entered no wars.
He made a peace treaty with Afghanistan.
He made a peace treaty between Israelis and Arabs.
He made a peace treaty between North and South Korea.
He entered into a secret alliance with Putin and Xi Jinping (not the CCP) against the enemies of humanity.
Donald J Trump appointed Commander in Chief of Nesara/Gesara.
Donald J Trump controls the New York Stock Exchange. Trump did not sign the Insurrection Act

after a fraudulent 2020 election to prevent a civil war in America.
Trump made peace with the Abraham Accord signed on 15th September, 2020.

Biden signed the Jerusalem Accord splitting Israel into two countries Israel/Palestine on 14th July, 2022.

A time period between Trump and Biden of 666 days. The Cern logo is 666. The Google logo is 666.

How do you fight the shadow FOURTH REICH?
QUIETLY AND SECRETLY.

President Trump and 209 countries shadow governments signed a peace agreement to introduce Nesara/Gesara.
The President is Commander in Chief of these countries.

WHY?

All these countries governments have been captured. The military established shadow governments in these countries.

WHO ARE THE ENEMIES

The enemy is the antichrist defined as Black Hats. The level of corruption is beyond imagination. Greed cannot be satisfied.

Satanic Cult ambition is to destroy Jesus Christ Bloodline.
Nazi Cult worship Satan, and wish to destroy mankind.
Communist Cult wish to destroy mankind.
Anti-GOD Cult wish to destroy mankind.

Worldwide criminal cabal, and mafia worship money, and exploit humanity. Mental and physical control; and greed are a driving force behind these inhuman individuals.

To expand on the Cults, history has provided plentiful evidence of their normal behaviour.

The Satanist hides and practices his black arts out of sight. Dennis Wheatley an author from the 1950's and 1960's wrote extensively on the black and white magic practiced by the followers of Satan.

The Nazis in Germany, gave their inheritance to history with World War 11, with their concentration camps and genocide of the inmates. The Communists exploded on the scene in 1917, and took control in Russia. There was much unrest until the 1930's when Stalin's imposed actions on the population which caused crop failures, famine, and millions died.

The Revolutionaries in China took control in 1911, and this resulted in the deaths of many Chinese in the years to follow. The Chinese Communist Party was formed in 1921, and after a massacre of communists in 1927, a civil war began between the Chinese Nationalist Government of Chiang Kai-shek and the Communists. This war lasted from 1927 to 1949 the communists being led by Mao Zedong.

The old Nationalist government leaders fled to Taiwan in 1947.

China today still violates civil rights, especially with the Uighurs, and the anti-COVID measures.

These anti-COVID measures exist around the world, held in reserve for the next bio warfare attack.

The Anti God Cult can be seen in their wokeism, pursuit of abortion, and gender manipulation desires.

NEW WORLD ORDER – TOTALITARIAN WORLD CONTROL

Ambition: to establish a One World Government.
Ambition: to reduce the population from 8 billion down to 500 million.
Ambition: to control world natural resources, and all assets. Create great man made global warming tax hoax.
Global reset planned.
Global slave society planned.
Global famine planned.
Global control by banning nitrogen fertilizer in farming.
Global disruption of oil production, transport, and energy.
Global nuclear war planned.
Global poisoning of food.
Global euthanasia and asset stripping of mentally ill, older population, and trouble makers.

Job vacancies available, submit CV to PO BOX 666, Gitmo.
The CAP 27 World Government Summit held in Glasgow 2022 now admit the existence of the New World Order, it is now FACT.

WORLD ECONOMIC FORUM – HEADQUARTERS SWITZERLAND ANNUAL DAVOS CIRCUS.

The new Technocratic World Order talk by Professor Simon Huntington of Harvard University

The Davos Class have little need for National Loyalty, view National Boundaries as obstacles that are thankfully vanishing, and see National Governments as residues from the past, whose only useful function is to facilitate the elite's global operation.

That is clear!

THE GREAT NEW DEAL

You will have nothing and you will be happy.
You will have something if you have your vaccinations.
We can switch your electric car off.
We can switch your mobile phone off.
We can switch your embedded chip off.
We can rehouse you.
We can charge carbon taxes to add a new income source.

We will introduce 5G and 6G towers to control your mind.
We will hospitalize and euthanise you when we choose

THE GREEN NEW DEAL

We will control your food supply.
We will genetically modify your grain.
We will genetically modify your meat in GM heat resistant cows. We will genetically modify your baby milk.
We will poison your processed food.
We will control your farmland available for production.
We will poison the soil with self-replicating nanotech.
Nanotechnology toxicity destroys the lungs, other organs, the brain, alters DNA.
We will destroy food production to create famine.
We will adulterate, control your water to create droughts.
We will hospitalise and euthanise you when we choose.

THE GREAT CURRENCY RESET.

What forms the new digital one world currency?
You will have a microchip between your thumb and forefinger.
You will have track and trace.
You will lose your job without the chip.
You will lose your right to purchase food without the chip.
You will have your trips curtailed by your phone messages.
You will give up your gun or your card will be frozen.
You will be given a social credit rating – ESG!
You will be vaccinated in accordance with W.H.O. edicts.
You will be given compulsory booster vaccines.
Your DNA will be altered, and you become a drug patent.
You will be given a free transfer to a concentration camp.
You will be given new cancer inducing vaccines.
We will hospitalise and euthanise you when we choose.

Klaus Schwab's Motivating Speech to the World's Economic Forum Young Global Leaders is:

"The young generation, like Prime Minister Trudeau, half his cabinet, are actually young global leaders, of the World Economic Forum. We penetrate the Cabinets. The change is not just happening, the change can be shaped by us. We have to prepare for an angrier world. How to prepare, take the necessary action to create the fairer world, I see the need for a great reset. The people assume we are just going back to the good old world which we had, and everything will be normal again. This is a fiction, this will not happen. There is only one way this pandemic is going to go, it is going to get worse, and worse, and worse. The next crisis is already waiting for us around the corner, and it's the climate crisis."

BLOODLINES
– SATAN FAVOURS HIS BLOODLINES

JESUS CHRIST

Jesus Christ was married to Mary Magdalene, and Mary and Joseph had other children, so Jesus had siblings. Satan has been looking for the offspring of Mary and Joseph, and Jesus's offspring since he was crucified.

AMERICAN PRESIDENTS

All American Presidents, except Martin Van Buren 8th, and Donald J Trump 45th, can trace their ancestry back to King John of England.

ROTHSCHILDS

Hitler is a bastard son, he fled by submarine to Paraguay in 1945.
Angela Merkel is allegedly his daughter.
Barack Obama is allegedly his grandson.
Greta Thunberg is allegedly the great granddaughter of Lionel Walter Rothschild.

CROWN OF ENGLAND

London Bridge is down. The Queen is dead. Her Lord Chancellor broke his Hollywood "WAND" and placed it on the Queen's coffin in Westminster Abbey.
From THE BIBLE: The Harlot is Running the Beast. The devil goes by 1,000 different names.

The Catholic Relief Act of 1829 places Catholics on a par with Protestants to be appointed to the sovereign as Lord Chancellor. The sovereign, however, is empowered to transfer the Lord Chancellors' ecclesiastical powers to the Prime Minister, or another Minister.

The Queen represented the Luciferin presence on earth. Both the white and black popes were subservient to her, but the Queen was subservient to the City of London, and the Rothschilds. The Queen had to remove her shoes in their company in the City of London.

Birmingham Commonwealth Games on 28th July, 2022, opening ceremony was a Satanic Showcase with a 10 metre high BULL OF BAAL, which was an exhibit on the Parade. The Council have been asked to find it a permanent home. The Bull is the subject of many old religions, not relevant in a Christian Society.

DEFINITION OF A KING

Under our Legal System, the Monarch, currently King Charles 111, as Head of State, owns the superior interest in all land in England, Wales, and Northern Ireland. This means all freehold property reverts to the King if there is nobody to inherit the property.
The Queen owned 287,000 acres around the UK.
The British Crown legally owns 6.6 billion acres across the world. That is one sixth of the earth's surface.

The sovereign is the Source of Justice, can do no wrong.
The sovereign has Immunity from Prosecution.
The sovereign is Supreme Governor of the Church of England.
The Sovereign pays no Inheritance Tax.
The Sovereign pays no Income tax, but now pays it voluntarily.
The Sovereign is never separated from his teddy bear, and toilet seat whilst travelling. I suspect that

more of his habits will become exposed to public scrutiny.

Long live King Charles 111, Commander in Chief of the Armed Forces, which are now seconded to the New World Order, One World Government, and World Economic Forum.

The latest news seems to be that Magna Carta is being analysed to see if it fits current events. All our MP's have pledged allegiance to a founding member of the World Economic Forum, so have become traitors to their nation and the people, as has the armed forces.

In the eyes of the law, ignorance is not an excuse, corruption and Kingly Rules apply.

Naturally, he will inherit his mother the Queen's responsibilities, subservient to the City of London, and controlling the Vatican Popes! Will he?

Thankfully, the armed forces have not pledged allegiance to the King. Charles 111 is under military control, is he now wearing an ankle bracelet?

King Charles had to appear as a witness on the 1st November, 2022, at an International Natural Tribunal Court of Common Law in Brussels. The Tribunal is for Queen Elizabeth 11 and the Duke of Edinburgh for crimes committed against humanity. Zoom will keep the hearing private.

King Charles 111 indictments unsealed on 4th October 2022? There could be charges against King Charles 111.

The Saxon – Coberg family are German, and not a British Royal Bloodline. Queen Elizabeth 11 and Prince Philip were cousins of the Saxon Coberg bloodline. Family changed their name to Windsor, and are controlled by the Rothschilds. This is known, so we are ruled by a false bloodline.

His brother, Prince Andrew, is a model of immorality.

Camilla and Charles' eldest son, Simon Charles Dorante- Day (56), in Queensland, Australia has had a DNA test so challenges lie ahead. Is that a pun, I wonder?
Simon Charles Dorante – Day is claiming to be the correct Prince of Wales.

Camilla and Charles' son was born in Portsmouth, and stayed with his mother for 8 months until adopted. Camilla at the Queens funeral was wearing a face mask, who is she?

Investigation has proved that King Charles 111 is not of the Royal Bloodline. Queen Elizabeth and the Duke of Edinburgh had false claims to the Crown.

There is proof that the Royal Line of King Richard 111 is corrupted. 1441 – King Edward 1V was born, a bastard line through King Richard 111 wife sleeping with an archer. How can I say that?

Well King Richard 111 was at war in Pointier in France in the summer of 1441. Prayers were said for him in the English Cathedrals, faithfully recorded in writing and dated proving that he was in France. Sadly, his wife could not wait for his return. 38 weeks later, the truth was revealed to the world.

There is hope here, because today, a claimant to the throne of England is King Michael, a resident of Jerildie in Australia.
My favourite is Charles will abdicate. The obvious choice is King William, whose father is allegedly

King Juan Carlos of Spain. Diana and King Juan Carlos of Spain are valid royal bloodlines.
There is a public petition on Change.org to strip William of the title of Prince of Wales. Is this to make room for Simon Charles Dorante – Day?

Nostradamus made a prophecy in 1555. The Queen would die in 2022. The next King will be Prince Harry, under the title King Henry 1X. James Hewitt and the future Queen Megan are looking forward to the promotion.

The real royal bloodline is the Spencer family, hence Charles marriage to Diana. It has been said that Princess Diana's bloodline goes back to Mary Magdalene and Jesus Christ. Her brother Charles Edward Maurice Spencer is a contender for the throne.

It is said that Diana is alive, and has old and recent photographs of herself on the Telegram Channel. Her modern day photographs support the view she is alive and well. There is a rumour that Diana did not agree to a divorce from Charles.
I thought about a visit to the bookies to see what odds I could get on a bet.

This has the appearance that our Lord GOD is removing the Aristocracy. They pursue behaviour to prove to their people that they are corrupt, and with power are dangerous. The dynasty of arrogant Lords and MP's has passed.

Strip them of their fancy dress, they are the same as the deplorables.

The Epstein, Ghislaine Maxwell story will be revealed. Epstein inherited the Hugh Hefner playboy empire within the C.I.A. Blackmail, bribery, sex and child trafficking, child satanic ritual and drugs were part of his everyday activities at his island in the Caribbean. Megan Markle is part of that corrupt circle.

Man and woman (with a womb) should divert attention away from false idols to walk with GOD, and the Lord Jesus Christ at our side. Trust in man is destroyed. Take your phone in switched off mode, and talk to GOD. He is listening.

VATICAN
– SATAN USES WEAPONS OF DECEPTION

WHY DO I SAY THAT?

The Vatican has three popes, white pope, black pope, and grey pope. The white pope is a Satanist that worships Satan in the light. Black pope is a Satanist that worships Satan in the dark. The black pope is a Jesuit, and controls the other two. Frie (friend) in German, Freemasons in English are under his control.

Grey pope is the administrator in charge of Vatican activities.

Look at the Protestant Bible, Exodus 20 verses 2 to 17
"Though shalt not make unto thee any graven image."
Look at the Catholic Bible, Exodus 20 verses 2 to 17
"You shall not make for yourself an idol."
The wording is very redacted in this instance but the meaning is clear.

Why then does the Catholic Church bow down to and worship an idol? Mary; mother of Jesus Christ.

This is in direct conflict with the word of GOD.

Dictionary Meaning: Priest
Official minister of non-Christian religion,
Inherited from pre-Christian era.

Jesus and the Jewish faith believe in reincarnation. In AD 553 Emperor/Pope Justinian excised reincarnation from faith. Their reason? The Oligarchs of the day promised to donate to the church in the next life, preserving their riches for their return.

The Catholic Church has removed 14 books from the bible, including the book of Enoch.

There is a Satanic Temple beneath the Vatican. There is also a new building built in 1970 that looks like the head of a snake.

Satanic Temple also exists below Buckingham Palace, and Washington DC, White House.

CERN, W.H.O. and W.E.F. headquarters in Geneva are all 6.66 miles apart.

Sadly, good Catholics are being misled by a corrupt leadership. No matter, GOD can distinguish between good and evil. A price will be paid there is more to be said.
The Vatican has the highest crime rate in the world. Tourist robs tourist.
The Catholic Church owns 177 million acres across the globe. This compares to 270, 000 acres owned by Bill Gates, and 50,000 acres owned by MacDonald's.

The Vatican has one of the largest telescopes in the world, in Safford, Arizona, USA, and it was once called Lucifer. The dark shows its face again.

No one is born in the Vatican State, only after you are appointed an employee of the Vatican are you granted citizenship.

BEHIND THE CURTAIN.

The American Inland Revenue Service tax funds are sent directly to the Vatican Bank to launder into Black Hat Projects.
The Vatican Bank handles the proceeds of money laundering, organ trafficking, human and child trafficking, opium, fentanyl, adrenachrome

trafficking, anything corrupt. Satanic child and human sacrifice rituals, and worship paedophilia in the church, not exclusive to Catholicism.

The Satanists have to publicize their intent in advance of action. Today, Hollywood provides the answers, enabling fictional plots to be turned into a Satanist style movie which projects their future plans. “The Simpsons” cartoons project future events at a cartoon level, and the deplorables laugh, and do not believe it.
Advanced notice has been given!

Lucifer seeks a secret police force to control the population. How does the black pope control the masses?
Battle for the mind, alter your thinking, symbolism. The Gestapo forces utilised are Knights Templar, Freemasons, C.I.A., F.B.I., Mossad, Antifa, B.L.M., M.I.5, M.I.6, G.C.H.Q., Police, Army, and many other militant forces.

The Georgian Guidestones were erected in 1979, and opened in 1980. It is close to Atlanta, in Alberton. They were erected in granite, 20 feet high, in 4 vertical pillars with a capstone. The granite assembled was an astronomical calendar.

It is inscribed on the faces in 8 languages, with 10 guides for humanity. The sponsor was anonymous, only known by a false name of R.C. CHRISTIAN. One of the ten guides for humanity rules is:

CIVILISATION SHOULD MAINTAIN HUMANITY AT 500 MILLION PEOPLE ON EARTH IN PERPETUAL BALANCE.

On 11th July, 2022, one of the columns was destroyed by an explosion. For safety reasons, the rest has been destroyed, and is now rubble.

The Georgia guide-stones were constructed 666 miles from the UN Building in New York.

The Statue of Liberty will fall? Prophecy made by GOD to be fulfilled.

The Obelisk at the Vatican will fall? Prophecy made by GOD to be fulfilled.

There is also a prophecy that the Vatican will be destroyed, timing and nature unknown.

THE GENERALS PATIENCE PAID OFF.

In 2016, the American elections were interfered with by the Vatican. The Italian government were informed and reluctantly gave in to USA pressure and allowed USA and Italian Special Forces to invade the Vatican. What an Aladdin's cave.

650 American Military Transport planes were needed to remove the gold from the Vatican tunnels covering hundreds of miles.

The gold from the twin towers was carefully stored, as well as everyone else's stolen gold, recorded meticulously by the scribe.

It has been stated that 640,000 metric tonnes of gold was recovered. At US $2,000 an ounce, that amounts to $45,150,720,000,000 in value, or US $5,644 each for the 8 billion people on earth.

Also, all books of historical interest have been confiscated.

Much more gold has been found in the tunnel systems elsewhere. Uganda has 31 million tonnes of gold in the ground and the United Nations want it.

Who owns and controls the United Nations?

There are four D.U.M.B.'s surrounding the Vatican which were on fire on 12th July 2022.

The Vatican, at the end of August 2022, put out an edict that all papal funds worldwide were to be transferred to the Vatican Bank by 30th September, 2022. Cash flow problem?

I am awaiting the main stream media catching up with the big news stories of the day.

This is a case of the Black Hats controlling the narrative is working against them, and works for the White Hats.

Crown controlled Vatican, Crown controlled USA Inc.
The Church of Rome and the Church of England are amalgamated and singing from the same hymn sheet.

Donald J Trump has exposed and shut down the organised theft.

POPE BENEDICT XV1 – from 19TH April 2005, to 28th February 2013.

Joseph Ratzinger was born on the 16th of April 1927, and died on the 31st of December 2022. He was born in Marktl, Germany, and was elected Pope Benedict XV1, from 19TH April 2005, until he retired on the 28th of February, 2013.

The "World Day of the Sick" is an observation that was started by the late John Paul 11. Benedict XV1 resigned as Pope at 8.00 pm on that day, the 11th of February, 2013. On that evening, lightning struck the Vatican from Heaven, an apocalyptic event, dictionary definition – describing, or prophesying the complete destruction of the world.

In 2023, a Private letter, which had been written by the retired Pope Benedict XV1 in 2015 to Vladimir Palko, a Slovakian member of an underground Catholic Church was partially disclosed to the public.

The tone of the letter suggested that the retired Pope Benedict XV1 believed that we are living in the time of the Antichrist. This must be considered the Last Testament by the retired Pope Benedict XV1 dated 2015, in the reign of Pope Francis.

"As one sees the power of Antichrist spreading, one can only pray that the Lord will give us mighty shepherds to defend HIS CHURCH against the power of evil in this hour of need."

Pope Benedict XV1 died on the 31st of December, 2022, which is the Saints Day of St. Silvester, the first Imperial Pope of Rome. The Roman Emperor Constantine recognised the Church and gave great gifts to St. Silvester.

This suggests that the reign of Imperial Rome, as the centre of the Church of Rome may be over. A history of scandals by the men who call themselves shepherds, bishops, pastors, and priests, are really wolves in sheep's clothing.

There exists a 300 page dossier on the Vatican leaks scandal, identifying the underground sexual activities amongst the clergy, and corruption within the Vatican Bank. It is suggested that this is what prompted Pope Benedict XV1 to resign, as it was beyond his ability to control.

The majority of Churches today have become servants of the State (Government) and need to break free. The Church of God needs to find its own voice, and criticise Non-Christian Activities by the State (Government) preach loudly from their pulpits, and call on the support of the people.

The Church of God needs to light a fire against Apostasy, which rules the State (Government) and inflicts it on the population.

Cardinal Camerlengo Torcisio Bertone destroyed Pope Benedict's "Ring of Fishermen" and the lead seal of Benedict's Pontificate. Benedict, in retirement, wore a regular ecclesiastical ring.

CROWN AND CITY OF LONDON

They owned Canada, Australia and the USA, until challenged by Donald J Trump in 2016.

Crown and City of London in business matters are buried in Kingly corruption for many centuries, which passes from one generation to the next. The City of London is working as the financial centre of the Cabal.

The following institutions, or instruments of the Crown, are working against their citizens.

Parliament, House of Commons, and House of Lords,
Crown Court System is a Corporation controlled by the Crown. Police System is a Corporation controlled by the Crown. City of London is a Corporation controlled by the Crown and incorporates the Metropolitan Police.

Roman and Admiralty, Maritime Law controls the legal system, Judges, Court Lawyers, Solicitors administering Maritime Law.
GCHQ, MI5, MI6, FBI, CIA, Mossad, Bank of England, a bankrupt Corporation, Pension Fund

completely empty, are all functionary independent bodies acting on behalf of the Crown.

Similarly, the Central European Bank, and Bank of International Settlements are both bankrupt. We are just waiting for the fall of the current banking system.

The worldwide quantitative finance system is now able to take control. It relies on the Elon Musk Starlink Satellites, which are operated by Elon Musk's SpaceX, providing internet access coverage to 40 countries as at end of 2022. It aims for a global mobile phone service after 2023.

There are many other NGO's supporting the CROWN, and there is definite evidence of concerted collusion between big business and big government working against the population.

Bank of England is a Private Bank, with a Crown granted authority to issue fiat currency. The paper is worthless, released by the Bank of England charging interest to the Government. All currency is immediately Debt to the Government upon issue, paid back through Government Authorised Tax Instruments on the people.

You will be happy to note that those with privilege enough to be called citizens owe the Government £64,000 to enable the Government to pay off its debts.
Fortunately for illegal migrants, they have no responsibility for this debt, and are granted more benefits than our own homeless people.

The House of Commons and House of Lords have acted irresponsibly.

How will today's children inherit and pay off such a bill, for profligate and corrupt expenditure, by irresponsible Governing.

The above operates in the USA as the Federal Reserve Bank, and is described elsewhere.

In August, a fire occurred under London Bridge, suggesting that a deep underground military bunker was under attack.

Boris Johnston is an actor fulfilling a role for the World Economic Forum to fool the uninformed. His successor Truss is a member of the W.E.F. and did not survive a political attack against her. Sadly, her successor, Sunak, is also deeply entrenched in the

W.E.F. Young Leaders mind altering indoctrination and fulfilling the role dictated to them by the W.E.F. Who is next in the queue, I wonder?

The House of Commons and House of Lords appear to be W.E.F clones of each other preaching the dictates of a satanic, communistic, Nazi, fascist agenda.

The words of the DALEKS come to mind
EXTERMINATE, EXTERMINATE, EXTERMINATE.

Especially linking their desire to lock down society and impose murderous vaccines on the people, through a less than independent health service bullied and bribed £15.00 per vaccine to the doctor.

The outcome has been disastrous on health around the world, and the guilty need to be called to account.

The World Economy has been slowly collapsing, and it is thought it will finally commence in London. This is in progress, we do not have an independent governing party, we have conservative and labour in bed with the World Economic Forum.

The Queen's death was finally recognised on 8th September, 2022. King Charles 111 is the W.E.F. representative in the United Kingdom. King Charles is the head of the Church of England, but he has no allegiance to GOD. He is a believer in genocide and destruction.
King Charles 111 cannot be allowed to carry out the W.E.F ambitions. Their plan is to destroy farming, agriculture, food production, and confiscate land and housing from the people. Genocide, through starvation, homelessness, and concentration camps.

Euthanasia plans for the mentally ill, and the elderly. This has already been legislated in the UK Parliament. Royal Assent will not be withheld. It would be an exemplary example if King Charles 111 volunteer's to be the first euthanasia patient.

Many Members of Parliament have already pledged allegiance to the W.E.F, and have now pledged allegiance to King Charles 111.

We, the people of the United Kingdom, have been betrayed. This is not as disastrous as it looks,

because King Charles 1st was executed in 1649 by hanging.
Treason against the People is the charge that King Charles has to answer.

There are many in power that are actors, the main corrupt character removed. This was done to expose the deep state operatives working for the W.E.F agenda. There is much respect for the Queen, but much was done by and in her name, which no normal human being would be proud of.

WASHINGTON D.C.
INC. IS A CORPORATION AND HAS ITS OWN LAWS

Donald's most famous quote is **"YOU'RE FIRED."**

In 1790, 16th July, Washington DC was founded by the signing of the Residence Act. The City of Washington was founded in 1791 to serve as the national capital, 100 square mile area. The founding fathers established the Constitution, and the Bill of Rights.

In 1860 to 1865, USA had a civil war, which bankrupted the country.

1871, Self-Governance was granted to Washington D.C.
This meant a similar tax free status as the City of London.

What history does not tell you is the tax free status was established because the corrupt bankers loaned money to the bankrupt government of the USA in exchange for the 100 square mile area and buildings on it granting equal status as the City of London, and the Vatican.

USA Inc.: A Citizen is an employee, and the company is registered in Washington DC Inc., and the City of London, which are foreign enclaves with their own laws.

President Woodrow Wilson 1913 – 1921 led America into World War 1 to make the world safe for Democracy.
The four organisations in which he supported their introduction in 1913 are:
FED: Federal Reserve Bank.
F.B.I.: Federal Bureau of Investigation.
I.R.S.: Internal Revenue Service.
A.D.L.: Anti-Defamation League.
A massive attack was made on Human Rights and the Constitution.

The company controlling Washington DC from 1871 was United States of America Incorporated. A separate company for each state. The 1871 USA INCORPORATED ACT of the United Kingdom Parliament was reversed by the British Parliament in 2022.

The USA Incorporated was reversed by Donald J Trump when he became President as in 2016, he re-introduced the American Constitution and Bill of Rights, cutting the Cabal companies off from their corrupt money supply.

Officially, United States Incorporated is bankrupt, closed for business, its assets owned by Donald J Trump. Washington DC is empty, the office buildings empty.

The Federal Reserve and the 12 Central Banks in America went bankrupt on the 13th September 2022.

The list of corrupt organisations in Washington DC is immense. These organisations work for the banksters that own and control them, with the exception of the first three listed who fund them through the Federal Reserve Fiat Dollar scheme.

PRESIDENT: Executive Branch of Government.
Joe Biden died in 2019 in Bethesda Maryland National Naval Medical Centre. – ask Alexa!
Biden's death, and the substitute false Biden, played in the beginning by his brother, and others with face masks makes the current USA Government illegal.

CONGRESS: Legislative Branch of Government, and SENATE: HOUSE OF REPRESENTATIVES – Senators of Both Congress and Senate are represented by Republicans, Democrats, and Independents.

Most Senators have been corrupted to the dictates of the World Economic Forum.

SUPREME COURT 9 Judges Exist to keep, the Executive and Legislative, parts of Government, in check within the Constitution. This has not been the case for some time as the Supreme Court of the United States is currently corrupted. Rule of Law is being re-introduced, but it is very slow, and currently reversed.

The Democratic Party have recently press ganged another 10 Supreme Court Judges into the Office of the Supreme Court with extreme LBGTQ+ views to determine all future Supreme Court rulings will be in accordance with the World Economic Forum dictates.

FED: US FEDERAL RESERVE BANK: A CABAL ORGANISATION.

FED lost the Charter to print US Fiat Dollars on 4th July 2022. Arrests have been made of people trying to print dollars after 4th July 2022.

CB: CENTRAL BANKS – Cabal Organisation.
Officially bankrupt 13th September 2022.

FBI: FEDERAL BUREAU OF INVESTIGATION
CABAL COMPANY WEAPONISED.

FBI is guilty of stealing inventor's patents over many years
It is known that 6,000 patents have been recovered by the white hats in their investigations. These have been suppressed and stolen over many years, which are beneficial to, but withheld from humanity.

Many invented by Nicola Tesla, who passed away in 1945. "Rods from GOD" (False name) was one of these major inventions. Another is "Medbeds" technology, which is a game changer for human health and treatment. The technology uses energy healing, quantum healing,
It will cure cancer, and many other illnesses.

Big pharma will go out of business with these advances.
Free energy devices, also engines that run on water Antigravity devices and time travel with Nicola Tesla.
This is very advanced technology from advanced alien peoples.

The FBI are acting outside the law with regard to their investigations and actions.

I.R.S.: INTERNAL REVENUE SERVICE INC – Weaponised

Company Registered in Porto Rico,
28th October 2017 Donald Trump issued an Executive Order shutting down the Internal Revenue Service in the USA, and providing all citizens with a full tax refund.
Gematria is used extensively by Satanists to calculate dates. This is also used by GOD and man to turn the tables on Satan.
If we add 1776 days to 28.10.2017, what date do we have?
The Queen died on 8th September, 2022, is this a co-incidence?
The cord has been cut by the death of the Queen.

President Biden is recruiting 87,500 additional armed agents to recover revenue for the illegal and fraudulent cabal.

There are no Internal Revenue Service Tax Laws in America. Therefore, all enforcement is illegal.

NASA: NATIONAL AERONAUTICAL SPACE ADMINISTRATION – Operation Paperclip 1945

The American Government invited the top German scientific experts in space technologies, other areas of technology and undercover Nazis, where Germany was more advanced. This included areas of medicine, mind control, and other rather unsavoury research. They were absolved of their crimes against humanity, for political expediency and technical advancement. America wanted it all. Consequently, many top Nazis got a free pass, pay rise and a new beginning in America in 1945.

The Third Reich was not dead, it was adapting to changed circumstances, and a new identity, with all the advantages of the American Free Market Economy.

The old illuminati organisations worldwide, which had remained dormant during the war were re-awakened.

DOJ: DEPARTMENT OF JUSTICE – Cabal Organisation.

Washington DC Weaponised, January 6th 2020
Allegations of armed insurrection made. All people arrested are still in jail, without being charged, for nearly two years. Only arms found were on Capitol police, authorised and present on the 6th of January. Habeas Corpus suspended. Bail refused. Law abandoned.
Conditions in jail are inhuman solitary confinement. Accommodation unfit for human occupation. The impartial administration of the justice system is not available. Unusually cruel conditions is how the report describes the prison.

CIA: CENTRAL INTELLIGENCE AGENCY
CABAL COMPANY – WEAPONISED

CIA Headquarters has 14,000 staff and operates under Lake Geneva in Switzerland. Access is by underground train from the CERN HEDRON

COLLIDER facility, and submarine only. This is a Gestapo subsidiary of the Black Hat Organisation.

The CIA has 8 supercomputers in Langley, USA, referred to as Snow White, Doc, Grumpy, Happy, Sleepy, Bashful, Sneezy, and Dopey.

CDC: CENTER FOR DISEASE CONTROL PREVENTION
A CABAL ORGANISATION

There are two major lawsuits against the CDC, for Vaccine Mandates. The CDC Research misrepresented the truth with false data.

Staff of CDC sold their shares in January of 2020, on discovering the plans to shut down the economy. Reinvested in shares, that benefited from the lockdown in the economy. Lockdown in China moved to Italy to refine the USA lockdown.

DEA: DRUG ENFORCEMENT AGENCY
AGENCY controlled by the C.I.A.

F.D.A.: FOOD AND DRUG ADMINISTRATION
AGENCY is controlled by Cabal Companies.

The FDA has made the practice of HOMEOPATHIC Medicine illegal in the USA.
This will be copied elsewhere in the world, and a mother giving her son or daughter a saltwater gargle for a sore throat will suddenly become a prisoner of the State, in the eyes of the State, for her offence.
Protecting Big Pharma, and their Lapdogs is the Government's first priority.

N.I.H.: NATIONAL INSTITUTION OF HEALTH
AGENCY controlled by Cabal Companies.
Within this umbrella is NIAID.
CHRISTINE Grady is head of "N.I.H. BIO ETHICS"
This is the company that approves all drugs for the F.D.A.
She is the wife of Antony Fauci.
Are you starting to see the big picture?

N.I.A.I.D.: NATIONAL INSTITUTION OF ALLERGY AND INFECTIOUS DISEASES

Dr Anthony Fauci is the director –
Budget approved for 2022 US $63 billion.

In 1998, Dr Ralph Barrett, and Dr Jang Lee were funded by the N.I.H. Dr Ralph Barrett worked at the University of North Carolina.

A virus was taken from an alien species, and developed it as a biological weapon against man. The origin was conceived from an illegal benign alien virus, which was added to human lung tissue causing blood clots.

This was outsourced to Wuhan in China, and a patent was taken out to destroy lung tissue to commercialise the venture. The patent number is 10130701.
You were never sick, you were poisoned.

A paper was prepared by Dr Ralph Barrett in 2020, which stated that an antidote was developed as well.
Information was withheld and all research is paid for by the American taxpayer.
In 2020, Dr Schultz proposed using large doses of zinc, which stopped the virus from spreading. A research paper and video was produced in 2020.
Dr Vladimir Zelenko was red-pilled by Governor Cuomo of New York. Cuomo issued an executive order which blocked access to pharmacies, and

Corsodil, which would have prevented deaths. Delaying treatment caused further deaths.

All doctors are bullied, vilified, gagging orders were issued, and staff was dismissed. Medical profession abandon ethics, by centralised decision-making of treatment, by government officials with no medical knowledge, State and Medical bureaucrats who are following instructions given by their remote manipulators and influencers.

Antiviral and anti-inflammation treatment approved would have prevented hospitalization, the most effective treatment tailored for the patient.

“Ask Dr Drew.”
Dr Drew interviewed Doctor Vladimir Zelenko, who researched COVID-19. Dr Zelenko’s conclusion was that COVID-19 was a weapon of mass murder, he reverse engineered COVID-19 to find the truth, and considers this action as the worst crime in human history. This was carried out as “GAIN OF FUNCTION” research, but is the opposite. The corona virus was modified to make it infectious and destructive to humans.

FEMA: FEDERAL EMERGENCY MANAGEMENT AGENCY
Controlled by the Cabal.

EPA: ENVIRONMENTAL PROTECTION AGENCY
Weaponised by United Nations: A Cabal Organisation.

Insanity is doing the same thing time after time, and getting the same result.

COP NR 1 TO COP 27 has maintained the global warming hoax whilst failing to save the planet.

NATO: NORTH ATLANTIC TREATY ORGANISATION.
A Cabal Organisation.

US AID: CHARITABLE AID NGO, A CABAL ORGANISATION.
W.H.O.: WORLD HEALTH ORGANISATION (owned by Bill Gates)
UNICAF: UNITED NATIONS CHILDRENS FUND
A Cabal Organisation.

H.R.H.: HUMAN RIGHTS WATCH
W.V.I.: WORLD VISION INTERNATIONAL
I.R.C.: INTERNATIONAL RESCUE COMMITTEE.

G: GREENPEACE
D.R.: DIRECT RELIEF
S.T.C.: SAVE THE CHILDREN – A Cabal Organisation for child kidnapping, and exploitation.
W.W.F.F.N. WORLD WIDE FUND FOR NATURE
A: AMERICARES
S.P.: SAMARITANS PURSE
SETI: Search for Extra Terrestrial Intelligence

Approximately 1.5 million non-governing organisations operate in the USA. The above are a small sample of the main ones. Many are funded by Congress, many controlled by criminal organisations. It is, therefore, a simple matter to launder money worldwide and traffic anything under the guise of charity, as there is no oversight.

RAND CORPORATION – USA GOVERNMENT INFLUENCER
Prepared report for Resident Biden, FBI, CIA, NSA, DNC, ON 22ND January 2022.

HOW TO DISMANTLE THE GERMAN ECONOMY?
1 – Shut down Russian Gas Supply
2 – Shut down French Nuclear power.
3 – American sanctions placed on Russia binding Europe to comply.

4 – Algeria cut off gas supplies to France.
5 – Blow up and destroy Nord Stream Pipelines 1 and 2
February 2022 Biden announced publically that the gas pipelines would be shut down.

Nordstream 1 and 2 gas pipelines from Russia to Germany was subjected to several undersea explosions on the 27th of September 2022. Biden accepted that he had done it? Dementia is talking the truth?

Result: EU collapsing, independence returning to individual countries?

It should be kept in mind that the depth of corruption in the rest of the USA and around the world is extremely difficult to determine because it permeates every corner of society, business, government, armed forces and non-governing organisations at all levels.

The worldwide mainstream media plays a large part in the pantomime, to maintain the propaganda of deception and lies with their false information stream.

The MSM is owned and controlled by 6 people, controlled by Reuters and Mossad, which in turn are controlled.

This implies that many, many, 1,000s are being employed to lie for and on behalf of their employers.

Many US and foreign companies participate in the scam for various reasons, to control the narrative, influence in a corrupt society, but mainly for greed money.

The governments and big businesses are funding the deception.

The Google operating system is called "adrena", and the software "chrome." Why? Adrenachrome is a drug produced from the blood of children. It is used in Satanic Rituals.
Facebook financed the corrupting of the election in 2020.

Twitter, too, was widely used by the FBI to influence the information available.

Chinese CCP participated through the voting machines and the worldwide web, in manipulating the election results.

It is reported that 600,000 people have been arrested in the USA, and 2 million worldwide. They are being held in offshore military bases, Gitmo, Guam, Greenland, Iceland, Crete, Tierra del Fuegu to name but a few. Many have been found guilty of treason in the Military Tribunals, and in some cases, replaced by clones or actors to maintain the facade of normality in their place of work.

It also enables the capture of many others within the chain of corrupt command.
NEWS UPDATE
2018 – DONALD RUMSFELD, DICK CHENEY, AND GEORGE BUSH JNR were arrested. They were transferred to Gitmo, and underwent a military tribunal, found guilty of treason.

I think a George Bush body double or clone was retained for eye candy, and not to alarm the rest of the rotting carcase of the Democratic, and Republican Party.

PSYCHOTHERAPISTS AND DOCTORS:

DECEIVERS AND SLAUGHTERMEN.

First, do no harm.

Hippocratic Oath has been prostituted for commercial gain. LBGTQ+ has brainwashed the weak minds to volunteer for experimental transgender alterations to their bodies.

We are sacrificing our children on the altar of malignant psychology. Radical transgender activists have taken over the dialogue. Extreme Satanists are indulging in child sacrifice, paedophilia, kidnapping, and trafficking.

Gender identities are established at birth, and the loud voices of the medical profession seek to commercialise a person's doubts. The bible has a solution: an eye for an eye.

These psychotherapists and doctors would reform, after the first transformation of a protesting doctor into the opposite sex. Or would they?

The Supreme Court of the United States overturned Roe v Wade, after a deathbed

confession by one of the parties, admitted that she lied to the Court 50 years ago.
The Abortion business has been severely affected by the reversal of the law. Young lives in the womb are being safeguarded by rescinding the previous legislation.
The birth rate has fallen dramatically since mRNA vaccine was introduced. Unexplained deaths have risen an enormous 40%, 84% in men between 18 to 39 years old.
Active malevolence controls these doctors and psychologists captive minds.

Doctors cannot be blamed for the chem-trails which pitch chemical poisons down on our heads, and viruses too.

CEO of PFIZER received 4 PFIZER COVID-19 vaccines, before catching COVID-19. There was no value, except monetary to the mRNA vaccine, since he caught it anyway.

It is known that mRNA vaccines alter human DNA, and would suggest an ulterior motive for the vaccine?

Ursela van der Layen was directly involved in a non-competitive negotiation of 1.8 billion dozes of PFIZER COVID-19 vaccine. Cost EU Euros 71 billion for delivery in 2023, and 2024.

This is a lot to pay, for a vaccine that does not work.

The EU European Medical Agency recommends approval of the COVID vaccine for infants aged 6 months and older. As at 20th October, 2022, 3 doses of PFIZER COVID vaccine for babies.

FDA refuses to release all medical files of people who died from the COVID 19 vaccines.

TRUDEAU is a shareholder in ACUITAS. ACUITIS licenced their mRNA delivery technology to PFIZER for the so-called vaccines. TRUDEAU is one of the main shareholders in ACUITIS which developed the lipid Nano particles for the vaccine. Poisons in a needle?

Every person that gets the jab is a payday for TRUDEAU. Further this implicates TRUDEAU in the murder of APOTEX owner Barry Sherman who produced a safe alternative. TRUDEAU is getting rich on injections.

The vaccine was produced in China prior to the release of the virus? It is recognised that the vaccine does not work, but not by the corrupt authorities wishing to control your mind.

Hence, vaccine, booster 1, booster 2, booster 3, booster 4, and then you are ill and die, having destroyed your immune system. Unless a friendly reptilian alien rescues your body: ulterior motive number 2. The real plan is to kill the human race, ulterior motive number 3.

The Florida Surgeon General has stated that the risk of death in males taking the mRNA vaccine by heart attacks is increased by 84% based on analysis of post vaccine deaths.

In Thailand, 391 children were given a health check prior to vaccination. Pre COVID, health check all children were healthy. After receiving the vaccine, all the children were given the same health check. Of the 391 children, 29.4% had developed post vaccine heart problems.

Denmark now states it is better and safer to have COVID-19, than to have the vaccine.

COVIDISM in Switzerland.

Those not vaccinated are being assaulted, there is a plan being tested in Switzerland to certify them mentally ill, and place them on a drug regime. Social contagion will create a new mental illness. Where has reason gone?
Actors will be employed to promote the BIG PHARMA desired outcome.

Dr Colin Campbell has been monitoring COVID-19 since the beginning. The doctors are paid £15 per jab. Dr John Campbell states in his studies patients would be better served by taking 4,000 units of vitamin D2 or D3 daily.

Also, K2 vitamins daily, which would save the NHS a fortune.

Doctors and Big Pharma make money out of prescriptions for "medicines", they do not make money out of grandma's old home remedies. Time to consult grandma.

Whichever way you look at it, you are reliant on the medical profession, hospitals, big pharma, and they die rich. Roll out the next pandemic, repeat with monkey pox.

N.I.H. and Wuhan developed, with apologies to the good aliens.

In Canada, Justin Trudeau, has already legalised euthanasia. The UK has similar laws.

A member of the Bilderberger Group Jacques Attali wrote a book in 1981: VERBATIM – Depopulation Agenda

Here is an example of the Elite's mind-set.

"The future will be about finding a way to reduce the population… Of course, we will not be able to execute people or build camps. We get rid of them by making them believe it is for their own good…We will find or cause something, a pandemic targeting certain people, a real economic crisis or not, a virus affecting the old or the elderly, it does not matter, the weak and the fearful will succumb to it. The stupid will believe in it and ask to be treated. We will have taken care of having planned the treatment, a treatment that will be the solution. The selection of idiots will,

therefore, be done by itself: they will go to the slaughterhouse alone."

WHAT HAVE THE GOOD ALIENS DONE FOR MANKIND?

DONALD J Trump funded Spaceforce, which introduced an independent information source, outside the supervision of the FBI, CIA and other captured spying agencies and organisations. Spying was taken to a new level, the spies were being spied upon.

The Spacelink Satellites have technology to provide:
Free Tesla Energy, power to mankind. Internet to mankind, uncorrupted and neutral, signal app required. Particle weapons can track and vaporise every nuclear weapon in its silo, within two seconds of its launch.

Much of this is all credited to Nicola Tesla, and Donald Trump's uncle, John Trump, who was a student of Nicola Tesla.

John Quincy Saint Clare, of the Hypersonic Research

Institute, invented the Philadelphia Experiments, authorities claim it as a hoax, but perhaps the authorities are hoaxing the deplorables.

John Quincy Saint Clare also invented time travel, as he was one. Time travel takes place through known portals. One location is under Cern in Switzerland, and the other is inside Cheyenne Mountain in Colorado, USA.

He holds patents for: Internet cellular prepaid phone services, walking through walls training system, remote viewing amplifier, full body teleportation system, internet accessible mailbox system, permanent magnet propulsion system, electrical dipole spacecraft, triangular spacecraft, photon spacecraft, and water energy generator.

All these devices are viable and hidden in the black and white hats arsenal. TR3B black triangular planes are built using advanced extra-terrestrial aircraft technology developed for US Inc. Government. It is 1,200 years more advanced than man's current design abilities.
Who provided the technology?

2020 USA FRAUDULENT ELECTIONS

The American elections were totally corrupt, and allowed to stand. Donald Trump and the General's action plans were passive, doing nothing.
Watch and we will catch them all, as the black hats implement their plans, which the white hats can disrupt, thwart, and arrest the traitors, should they chose, or let continue to wake the population up.

Dead people voted, still registered on the rolls. The Democratic Party has a very focused ballot harvesting team that seek out non-voters and offer to cast their vote for them. A new documentary, 2,000 mules, is now released giving details of the voting fraud. There is also two children's books, one called as above, and the other "Plot Against the King" available on the internet.

In 2020, the armed forces had been monitoring the elections, and knew the result had been subjected to fraud. Donald Trump was appointed Commander in Chief of the Armed Forces, and the NORAD Cheyenne Mountain Nuclear Central Command was locked down on 20th March, 2020. We are now at a Defcon one emergency alert level, in expectation of a nuclear war event.

The Biden Government must respond to Donald Trump's Emergency Acts. Three in all issued after the November 3rd election on 2020.

The reason there has been no response to Trump's executive orders, the Democrats are all guilty of treason, fraud, and crimes against humanity.

Military Law has been enforced, and arrests are taking place quietly, without creating a civil war in the nation.
The plan is set by GOD in Heaven, and told to His Prophets.

Recently, three States have decertified their 2020 elections, and the Sheriffs' are arresting the criminals.
There are three countries involved in the 2020 Election fraud, the Chinese CCP the main offender manipulating the votes remotely, also the Crown in the City of London, and the Vatican in Rome.

The Supreme Court of the United States has been provided with evidence. This has resulted in an overturning of the 2020 election result. A "Shadow Document" has been issued which maintains secrecy on this judgement. The reason: to prevent a premature uprising and civil war which the deep state and fraudulent government desperately desire to start.

It permits the Biden Residency and the deep state to dig all of them further into exposing themselves, and their plans, with the outcome bankruptcy. Economic collapse happens, highlighting crimes of treason and others.

Biden, the resident puppet, and his masters in power, needed to turn Trumps economic miracle upside down.

Trump, when in power as the President, took steps to devolve military power, away from the current fraudulent pretend President.

All efforts to expose the crimes have been quietly progressing through the Courts, from the lowest to the highest, exposing the corruption, to attempt to overturn in every State.

Sadly, the voting machines are in use worldwide, all connected to a central control within that country, enabling a false result to elections to be engineered.

There are 209 – 214 Countries with Shadow Governments waiting to enact Emergency Martial Law. Currently, the main action by the white hats is behind the scenes exposing the corruption. The main gatherers of intelligence information has been the Military around the world, as the recognised spying agencies are captured black hat operators.

The Great Reset was proposed by the World Economic Forum. A Parallel Great Revaluation was established by the White Hats on 1st September 2021, but which one has the upper hand?

2022 17TH NOVEMBER 2020 ELECTION CONTESTED.

Resident Biden Vice Resident Harris and 286 Members of Congress impeached, and the case has now reached the Supreme Court of the United States of America.

There are also another two prepared impeachment cases moving through the courts in case the first one fails.

2022- 8TH NOVEMBER MID TERM ELECTION

The USA midterm elections took place in November, most results are known with some being contested.
The result has given the Republicans the Majority in the House of Representatives after gaining more than 218 seats.
The Senate result is the Democrats have 49 seats, and tie with the Republicans' with 49 seats. There are 2 Independent's, whose vote is not allied to either party.
On 20th December, 2022, Kristin Cinema resigned as a Democrat, and informed the Senate that she is now standing, and will vote as an Independent.

The Vice Resident Harris has a casting vote which can be used in a tie. The Democrats at best can only tie the vote.

The above however is a charade.

1777 – 17th November Republic of America was established.
2022 – 17th November Republic of America was re-established.

2023 – January Director of Homeland Security Impeachment.
Senator Mayorkas Impeachment Trial begins.

All elected officials have been elected to a bankrupt Corporation USA INC.

New elections will have to be held to re-establish the Republic of America.

The above invalidates all members of Congress and the Senate. As they are part of USA INC., now bankrupt and struck off.

No Fly Zone removed from the White House.
No Fly Zone established over Mar A Lago.

USA Inc. is bankrupt, operating with the cash in the till.
USA Senate and Congress represent USA Inc.
Do not represent the Republic of the United States of America.

NESARA/GESARA LAWS will be followed to appoint a new government.

White House was being used for Military Tribunals for Treason Trials. The White House we see on TV is used by Hollywood.

A Worldwide Nuclear War scare will shut down the USA, and all the other countries, and the Military will mobilise and take control. All known deep state operatives still in place will be arrested.
Twitter has been taken over by Elon Musk, on 28th October, 2022. He carried a ceramic sink into the head office, and said "Let that sink in!"

There have been many disclosures of truth now from Twitter and Elon Musk, which is demonstrating the collusion and false propaganda. Many truth tellers have been banned from Twitter and are now being reinstated.

COLLAPSE OF ALL CURRENCIES

The Federal Reserve Fiat Dollar System supporting world trade is collapsing under the weight of debt in the world trade system.

The Federal Reserve is bankrupt, final on 30th September, 2022. The introduction of NESARA/GESARA ensures the total collapse of American domination of World Politics, and Economics.

This will probably cause an immediate imposition of worldwide Marshall Law... such a collapse will reduce the world to a short term breakdown of law and order until a new political government is elected to exclude the previous corrupt governments around the world.

A Prophecy, however, has been made that Donald J Trump will be reinstated publicly as President to serve out his term that was stolen in the rigged and illegal corrupt election in 2020. The next election will be held in 2028.

The corrupt will be arrested and pay the price for their treasonous actions against their country and crimes against humanity.

Biden's Executive Order 14067 of 9th March, 2022, introduced total control over all bank accounts in USA effective 13th December, 2022. This theft of your money will be controlled by the C.B.D.C. (CENTRAL BANK DIGITAL CURRENCY.) the Central Banks, however, are bankrupt, so this is bound to fail.

C.B.D.C – CENTRAL BANK Digital Identity to be imposed by the black hats, it will fail, thankfully, but much will be stolen by the Government until Nesara/Gesara is implemented.

October 8th, 2022 the democratic Jan 6th 2020 committee subpoena Trump.
November 7th, 2022 another attempt is made on Trump's life.
The power of prayer to our Lord will overwhelm Satan.

GOD IS WORKING TO FREE MANKIND FROM THE GLOBAL TOTALITARIAN POWER.

NESARA/GESARA

This revaluation was called NESARA/GESARA for National and Global coverage to be inclusive of all countries conditional on the following terms:
Countries introduce natural and common law for the people.
Peace with other countries.
Peace with own citizens.
Nuclear weapons must be discarded.

A gold backed currency to stabilize currencies, supported by silver, precious metals, and other commodities.

This Nesara/Gesara was firmly in place by the 1st of February, 2022, but remains dormant awaiting the collapse of the old currency system, the Fiat Dollar.

It was activated on the 1st of June 2020, and many corrupt black hat bankers got caught trying to do what they had always done without consequences.

The first country to adopt this was Zimbabwe, and the Brics countries; Brazil, Russia, India, China, and South Africa have joined too.
Many more are in the process of joining.

The scheme is administered through Elon Musks Starlink Satellites system, which was activated on 24th September, 2022.

A white hat plan of devolution is in place awaiting a controlled release, as the policy and regulations are introduced.

Gold 1 gram coins will be minted, and are now in circulation in Zimbabwe. These are in use instead of paper money. They have the same value around the world. Encryption to be devised using the quantum financial system together with quantum devices, which could be Tesla phones. Companies will operate within the quantum system. What about Currency under the mattress? Rumour suggests paper currency will remain for six years until a digital solution is found to comprehensively cover all issues. The whole operation is supervised by the Military worldwide.

The concept seems to be that all currencies will be revalued to be equal, but retaining their original country name. USA in Dollars, Russia in Rubles. This supports the theory that many currencies will rise in value, whilst many will fall. Payments made to the country must be made in the local currency. This presumably stops or reduces money laundering in foreign currencies.

The question now is which currency in a worldwide market will take down all the other currencies?

The USA Supreme Court, and all informed Government Public Officials in the Banking and Legal Systems in every State, conspired in 2010 to gag all information on Nesara/Gesara Treaty from the Population.

Nesara/Gesara will be released to the public in full on the 1st of February 2023, but may be delayed awaiting the collapse of the Cabal Organisation, and end of the war in Ukraine.

SECRET WORLD WAR UNDERGROUND

BETWEEN WHITE HATS, versus BLACK HATS AND ALIENS.

Alien Agenda – humanity has been enslaved for centuries by Satanic Forces in control, and Aliens in the Hives. The Alliance are fighting entire Battalions of Aliens.

The military worldwide has been carrying out a secret underground war for the last six years to neutralise and destroy the deep state and Alien military machine.

The battle above ground was carried out using COVID-19 bioweapons and vaccine needles using poison to alter human DNA, and attack the human heart.

The fighting underground was much more deadly using conventional weapons by the White Hats, and against the superior weapons of the Aliens and Black Hats.

These battles were fought in deep underground military bases, hives for the Reptilian occupants. They are all connected worldwide with underground tunnels at 10,000 feet and high speed maglev trains.

There are many ancient tunnels, which have been exposed by mining activities, like diamond and deep mines, all covered up, and denied by "Authority."

These tunnels were made with mazer microway Lazer Light, which vaporised the rock. Thus, no spoil was left on the surface.

The d.u.m.b., under Denver Airport in the USA, is bigger than Denver City on every level, and there are 8 levels.
The fighting must have been horrendous. Within these underground bases it is said there is enough food for 150 years.
Iceland, Scotland near Lochgilphead, and under Glasgow, New Zealand, Australia, Iran, Afghanistan, Pakistan Myanmar, Laos have d.u.m.b.s.

Many of these d.u.m.b.s are simply flooded as a means of destroying their inhabitants. It is a life saver, but a later investigation is required to ensure success. The d.u.m.b. at the White House was destroyed in this manner.
The Potomac River was diverted.

The Hoover Dam had a dumb hive underneath, but was found to be empty.

The Euphrates River has dumb hives underground, the old underground systems are being flooded.

There is a non-terrestrial presence in Ukraine, Devil Mountain? Location is unknown, and battles are ongoing between the Russian Special Forces, against Reptilians in many underground dumb hives, with competing AI Systems in play. The Illuminati believes the Devil resides in Devil Mountain. The bio laboratory research being done is on Slavic peoples.

There are nine pyramids in Crimea, and a highway, where vehicles are known to disappear underground. The Alien craft in full stealth mode can drive into mountains.

Crimea underground labs are processing Thorium, which is a radio-active metallic chemical element. It has a half-life of 14.05 billion years.

The Indus Valley in Afghanistan, Pakistan and India has hosted underground Aliens for millions of years.

Mexico has an ET presence, as has South America, through the presence of UFO's, and Grey ET's.

The maglev train system is worldwide, from the Antarctic, to New Zealand, South Africa and South America.

The main centres must revolve around the CIA headquarters under Lake Geneva, both a submarine tunnel to the Adriatic Sea, and a train tunnel running to the Vatican City exist.

The Vatican City has a tunnel running to Albania, (where another hoard of Vatican Gold was found) Greece, Ukraine, Crete, Libya, Tunisia, Monacco, and Gibraltar. Another goes to Jerusalem, and a third to Lake Geneva and the Alps.
Libya has a massive underground laboratory.

In America, all the deep underground military bases are connected, but they are so secret that many are not even known, that situation will apply around the world.

The New World Order is being slowly extinguished below the ground, preventing their rise in the future.

There is a submarine tunnel existing to take submarines from the Atlantic to the Great Lakes. Keep in mind Ghislaine Maxwell was a submarine captain.

There are 46 USA Inc. Biolabs in Ukraine being run by the Black Hats, supervised by Black and Veitch Company, financed by the Department of Defence. They are administered by Hunter Biden, son of the Resident.

These are for the development of man-made viruses to infect mankind, a repeat of COVID-19.

The d.u.m.b.s have and are home to a slave society, super soldiers, child and human trafficking, baby factories through captives, factories for the production of adrenachrome, human organs for transplant, and human flesh for the alien

occupants living below ground. Also, the research facilities for the reptilians and greys.
The USGS website provides information on the latest earth tremors or quakes. Examination of quakes at the 10 km depth provides a pattern showing, and indicating the direction of the tunnels at the 10 kms depth. They are being destroyed by "Rods from God" or flooding by the white hats worldwide.

The military shadow governments of the 209 – 214 countries co-operated to establish victory, but fighting continues in secret, and above ground, and the psychological/legal fight continues worldwide.

A JUST GOD is recovering his dominion over his people.

Satan and his demonic possessions have sought to take over the world since time began, but started again in 1945, when the Nazi's fell, but did not surrender.
Evil flourishes when good men do nothing!

These evil ones are being exposed, arrested, and taken to trial for crimes against humanity, and as traitors to their country.

GOD'S PROPHECIES

GOD's Prophets have risen as Satan grew stronger. They are defying Satan's Agenda, and announcing GOD's WORD, and action to bring his world back into balance. In the bible, money is and will be backed by gold. GOD's Prophets Robin and Robyn Bullock, Timothy Dixon, Amanda Grace, Hank Kunneman, Kent Christmas, Mario Murillo, Perry Stone, Troy Black, Julia Green, and others from the USA, and Rebekah Erland, from South Africa, have been extremely active in voicing the prophetic word from our Lord GOD in Heaven.

God issues his news before the news.
God through his Prophets has been describing extreme weather events well in advance of them happening. GOD's angels are at war.
In South Africa, the country is going to burn. Europe has extreme hailstorms, flooding have and will be experienced. Also, droughts in Sicily Mount Etna volcanic action took place. In Iceland, expect a volcano to erupt.

In London, expect Big Ben to fall?

In the case of the Queen, when she passed, a message was given that London Bridge had fallen down.
Is King Charles 111 involved in the death of the Queen?
Is King Charles 111 linked to other unacceptable behaviour?
We can only speculate at this time.

In Paris, watch the Eiffel Tower for a sign?
Struck three times by lightning, is that the sign?
In Belize watch for a sign?

In Saudi Arabia, extreme flooding took place.
In China, the 3 gorges dam is closed and being drained due to earthquake damage. Other dams are affected by extreme flooding.
In Hawaii, expect a volcano on Mount Kilauea to explode.
California is going to have snow in the summer.
The buffalo are fleeing Yellowstone Park, an earthquake is expected. The Park was closed to the Public for safety reasons. Prophecies are predicting an earthquake in California. Also in New York, undersea earthquake or tsunami event is predicted. The Appalachian Mountains are another area of earthquake predictions.

The Mississippi River will run backwards?

The Statue of Liberty and Washington DC will fall? Is this a political prophecy or a prophecy of destruction of buildings? The Abe Lincoln Memorial will survive.

In New York, on Liberty Island stands the Statue of Liberty. Lady Liberty is 151’1” high (46m), with a pedestal 305’ high (93m) built in 1886. Lady Liberty is based on the Roman Goddess Libertas, also known as the Greek Goddess Elyutheria. Goddess of Liberty given a temple on the Aventine Hill on Rome in circa 238BC. It is struck by lightning 600 times a year.

In USA/CANADA, the Niagara Falls will run with green water.
A prophecy was made that Washington DC would be hit with pestilence and plagues. Currently, Washington DC is hit with hepatitis, which is only striking down the black hats, turned by God, against the people who released it on to the community.

In Australia, massive flooding has been taking place around Sydney. In New Zealand, expect underground and undersea earthquakes.

In Japan, expect a typhoon, China invasion plans thwarted.

Iran has been paid by the USA (Obama) to start a nuclear war. There is going to be a nuclear war threat.
Bombings are to take place in Israel.
These are mostly global weather events, which are weather weapons, and biblical events demonstrating the power of our Lord GOD in Heaven.

There is a second revolution in America after the first of 1776. This needs to happen around the world to take back all countries, and bring Justice to replace the dictatorship imposed by Satan and his demonic possessions.

THE RISE AND FALL OF THE ONE WORLD GOVERNMENT

THE END OF THE GLOBAL TOTALITARIAN STATE.

Canada, USA, Central and Southern America, United Kingdom, European Union, Africa, Iran, Israel, China, Taiwan, Australia, New Zealand, and many other countries, still have to deal with the removal of their demonic politicians, and deep state operatives, that through blackmail, intimidation, or greed are controlled by the New World Order criminal empire represented by the World Economic Forum and their satellite companies and organisations peddling their satanic and communistic agenda.

Individual voters gave up consent unconsciously to their governments, and states, allowing the governments and states to legislate against them, to pursue a global agenda of world depopulation by any means.

The world as we currently know it is an artificial construct, carried out in an artificially created environment. The world as we know it is ending.

What needs to be done?

The following existing world systems have to collapse:
Financial markets, legal systems, political law enforcement, corporate business practices, pharmaceutical drugs and treatments industry practices, medical services, Hollywood, mainstream media, main social media, education, children, youth and university programmes corrupted, military occupation of foreign lands.

This has all come about through government legislated interference caused by corporate interests projecting manipulated solutions to benefit these organisations financially and for other more malignant reasons.

An introduction of sovereign law is a priority to make man equal to man equal to corporations.

All organisations seeking to manipulate influence must be shut down, and their officers answerable for crimes against humanity.

THE GROWING PAINS OF DISMANTLING THE ONE WORLD GOVERNMENT

The one-world governments are creating a chaotically disruptive effect on energy, mining, fertilizer, manufacturing industry, and farming. Diminished output is causing collapse on many levels, and food famine.
Costs will rise dramatically. The people will protest and strike and political unrest inevitable until a change in governments through martial law are achieved.

The monopolist bullies and corrupt governments must be removed, punished, imprisoned, and wealth confiscated.
They will have nothing, and they will be happy.

The world population will be happy after the removal of the carpet baggers.

ANSWERS

The world is collapsing the SWIFT Financial System, and replacing with the Quantitative Financial System. When the switch is flipped (False War

Alert), humanity will start anew. Secure systems are now in place awaiting the switchover.
Establishes world peace and redistributes the wealth of the world.

Military Martial Law will replace Maritime Law in the short term, and Common, Natural and Universal Law in the long term.

From MSM to Project Odin
From toxic drugs to Tesla Med Beds Sonic Healing
From fiat bitcoin, and currencies: to XRP cryptocurrency backed by silver.

SCAMS BEING PLAYED ON MANKIND BY GOVERNMENTS AND OLIGARCHS

The politics of the World Economic Forum and government is used to control supply, escalate prices. The politics of sanctions is in place to escalate prices.
Market prices are dictated at a world trade level. Local and regional prices do not dictate world prices.

Thatcher, in her time as Prime Minister, privatised energy because the market knows better than government how to generate energy competitively.

Corrupt that and apply the opposite rules, the market knows how to manipulate prices upwards to overcharge their customers, and tax laws enable the profits to be hidden. Since this market is a world market, the same pricing structure is applied around the world to allow for local variations.

To do that we have to pretend that we have a market; which is a pretend market.

1 - ELECTRICAL ENERGY MARKET

PRODUCERS AND GENERATORS

Coal, wood pulp, hydro, hydrogen, tidal, gas, oil, wind, solar, biomass, and nuclear power companies sell electricity to the wholesalers and suppliers. Power is produced from the above sources to generate electricity.

The various sources of electrical power generation have a variable minimum cost of generation, each different from the other. They all compete over the National Grid for market share.

CARRIERS OR POWER GRID

In the UK, it is the National Grid that has monopolistic authority, over the distribution of electricity. This situation exists in most countries of the world, which transfers the energy from the generator for the suppliers' point of need, the consumer.

In America, since the 2020 Election, to December 2022, it has been recorded that 102 attacks, by an unknown terrorist organisation, have been made against the USA National Transmission lines and sub stations in an attempt to shut down the electrical power.

CONSUMERS

They suffer from market manipulation because the most expensive producer marginal cost price of the producers, and National Grid is the ruling price applied to all domestic suppliers, which is used to calculate that domestic suppliers rates to consumers.

HOW THE SCAM WORKS

Every day, producers auction their supply, highest price wins, then, price is the same for everybody. The marginal maximum wholesale price becomes the minimum retail price. There is a mathematical formula for each type of production to adjust the tender price.
It is a government sponsored scam, needs legislation against price fixing and manipulation in the market and super profits. Governments are agents working for Oligarchs, and Power Companies.

The UK electricity output has allegedly a self-sufficiency in power: more than 50% electricity is from wind and nuclear, 35% of our electricity is from North Sea Gas, and 15% of our electricity is imported from French nuclear power.

There is no reason for such draconian price increases in retail supply charges. The infrastructure has not changed, therefore, the day rates for gas/electric supply increased prices are not justified. Solar power has no recurring costs after construction, cost prices should be based on cost plus 5% profit overall.

Costs of power would reduce prices by over 50%
The daily pretend auction of power (Stock Exchange)

The price for every produced megawatt is? It varies per supplier, EU $70.00 per year for wind power generated?
The price for every auctioned retailed megawatt is? EU $600.00. Is that the price of nuclear power I wonder?
This is easily manipulated on a daily basis.
The government is recovering say EU $500.00 per megawatt from the retailers, and granting nominal refunds, and a cap on retail bills. This say EU $500 surplus is then returned to fund the retail companies.

The above is working well in Greece, adopted by the EU and probably obtained the idea from the practice adopted in the UK.

There is also the escalating VAT recovery accruing to the Treasury, and an unknown amount of carbon tax element. The daily pretend auction will make up any shortfall to the suppliers.

The above, however, takes the consumers eyes off the obvious. Planned cuts at peak demand times. This will be recurring, resulting in much fridge and freezer foods being spoiled. Time clocks will have to be adjusted daily after every power cut. That may do nothing or just alter the disruption times.

Get your long forgotten thermal underwear out of your bottom drawer.

2 – OIL AND GAS MARKET

Governments are restricting the oil and gas industry to keep prices high, due to insufficient supply. Prices have risen dramatically impacting the common man's ability to pay the price.

Oil and gas industries are being sabotaged by an unknown terrorist element, causing a drop in supply, and consequential rise in price.

Pipelines planning permission are being withheld by governments, forcing fuels to be transported by rail, increasing costs, forcing prices up more. Railway oil transports are being derailed to delay deliveries, damage track and rolling stock.

Nordstream 1 & 2 gas pipelines from Russia to Germany damaged on the 27th of September 2022. President Biden has admitted that "He" authorised the sabotage of these pipelines in January 2022. Refer to the RAND REPORT that was described earlier within the heading WASHINGTON D.C.

A NATO/USA naval exercise took place during June 2022 in the Baltic Sea to test underwater drones. The area of the tests was the area of the explosions. It has also been disclosed that USA helicopters from a Polish/USA military base flew a mission out to the area of Nordstream 1 and 2, so perhaps were involved in the setting off of the previously installed drones/mines.
It is said Ukraine divers were trained by the USA Special Forces in underwater sabotage.

Norway announced within days of the explosions that it had opened a gas pipeline from Norway to Poland.

Israel is now seeking to reach a border agreement with Lebanon to drill for gas in the eastern Mediterranean. The plan is to supply gas through Turkey to Germany in a new pipeline, from the Karish Gas Field.

The Gas Pipeline between Russia through Ukraine to Europe has developed a leak on 21st December, 2022, in the Republic of Chuvashia in Western Russia, which has caused an explosion, killing three people and shutting down the gas supply. Was this sabotage?

The price of plastic has increased 350%.

UKRAINE/UN/NATO/MOSSAD/W.E.F. are on the same page. America now controls gas to the EU. Biden benefits from Ukraine gas to EU through his son's financial interest in Burisma.

Carbon dioxide (CO_2) can power the world. It is cheapest form of power available. Removal of carbon releases oxygen. More study required.
Children in the Czech Republic are attending school wrapped in blankets to keep warm, as the school heating is no longer functioning.

3 - NUCLEAR INDUSTRY

AMERICA – Hillary Clinton as Secretary of State approved the sale of Uranium One, the only Uranium Company in America, to Russia with Obamas approval in 2010. Rosatom in 2010 acquired a Canadian Company which had assets in the USA. Bill Clinton was paid US $500K to speak in Moscow after the purchase.

A further US $2.35 million was paid to a Canadian Foundation that the Clintons are involved with. Under Canadian Law, she cannot divulge the donation.

Russia acquired a 20% interest, but could not export the uranium from the USA. US $3 million was donated to the Clinton Foundation in a year. UEC – Uranium Energy Corporation bought back the mine in the USA in December 2021.

Uranium prices currently are US $38 per pound, and are expected to rise to US $100 per pound.

Germany has closed all its nuclear power plants. France has closed two plants, but is bringing them back on stream. American nuclear power is 20%, and 50% of the uranium is from Russia. Only Russia and China build nuclear reactors, Russia has 5% of the uranium production capacity, but controls 40% of the enrichment capacity.

France currently has 24 Nuclear Power Stations shut down for maintenance, so is undergoing a serious shortage of electricity. As 15% of the UK electricity comes from French Nuclear, it is almost certain to impact the UK supply.

4 – WIND AND SOLAR POWER

This source of power is considered to be less than 3% of the current world output of electricity. Wind is erratic, solar is erratic, in most parts of the world.

Wind farm blades cannot be recycled, and fires in the electric generators are common.

Solar panels have a lifetime of 20 years maximum, and require regular cleaning in a damp climate to prevent green mould build up covering the solar surface.

5 – VEHICLE MANUFACTURING MARKET

Engines burn more fuel than they should because the manufacturers and oil companies are complicit in the design. Fuel prices have increased 60% in the UK and 100% elsewhere.

The electronic chip market through sanctions has seriously impacted supply. Manufacturing cannot be completed because of the absence of a chip.
The new USA Infrastructure Bill authorises a kill switch installed into all new cars, which will halt a car instantly, and the driver will have no control.

The introduction of the E10 fuel, with Bio fuel content increased to make it "green". This will affect seals and shorten the life of the vehicle.

Electric cars are not the answer to the green world transport plan. In France, the Governmental civil service managers were given electric vehicles. Sadly, they have been scrapped. They all needed new batteries, and the old batteries cannot be recycled, nobody will buy the second hand vehicle. Battery prices are prohibitively expensive.

The uptake of electric cars by motor dealers is restricted to the major dealers, as the small dealerships cannot afford the equipment necessary to maintain and service an electric car, which costs about US $1.5 million.

That creates motor dealership monopolies. Only the large survive.
In the early years of WW11, a company called Ricardo's which still exists today, converted several British army vehicles to run on water. It is possible the paperwork and plans still exist in Ricardo's archives in Shoreham in West Sussex. The concept was abandoned in 1943 when oil based fuel supplies became widely available.

It is known that SHELL have a patent to convert water to fuel. There is a history of premature death or disappearance of people who invent water engines to run on hydrogen.
Stanley Myer invented a water engine, but his suspicious premature death brought the

technology to a halt. Patent created for an electronic process but it is incomplete.

The W.E.F want to save the planet, why are they not investing in the production of cheap bubble cars?

6 – WATER SUPPLY MARKET

Ground water is being pumped out of the ground around the world. Most of these sources have been commercialised by private companies. This water is all old, and once extracted, the ground becomes barren. Corporate man once again demonstrates he is out of control.

Water supply is under threat through drought. Lake Mead, Hoover Dam, Glen Canyon Dam threaten the power supply due to drought, and unrestricted use of the Colorado River water supply. Lake Las Vegas surrounded by golf courses has priority, and the industrial and farming community pay the price, stop production.
Basic water has gone bankrupt and the price of water in the area has skyrocketed. Las Vegas city is charging 500% more for the available water.

Euphrates River in Iraq is also in a severe drought situation, affecting the farming community.

The Three Gorges Dam has no water, stopped generating electricity. A 900 kilometre stretch of the Yangtze River has no water. Drought is here, and worldwide, but many places are being flooded by GOD to demonstrate that he is in control.

The Mississippi River water levels are so low, transportation of goods by boat is under threat. Water levels are reducing loads carried dramatically.

Big Corporations are today's pirates, in collusion with the Government to scam the world's resources.

Nestle do not consider people have the right to underground water. Nestle have bought water rights around the world, and sell it very expensively in bottles. Nestle pumps water out of various States in USA, Michigan, California into other States, leaving these areas in drought conditions. Nestle bottle tap water, and label it spring water. Every tank full of water costing US10 is bottled and sold for US $50,000.

Coca Cola are a similarly tainted Corporation. These companies are stealing water and selling it back to us.

What is the solution to the problem?
Antarctica can provide man's water requirements from the annual melt. Man needs to design a method to exploit it.

The N.W.O., O.W.G., World Economic Forum have planned a biological attack on the inside of the water system against America.

Heavy metals, lead, and fluorine are in the water to poison man. Flint, USA, water flowed in lead pipework. Water poisoned the minds of children and adults alike.
Fluoride is a neuro toxin and dangerous to humans, it softens the teeth. Fluoride in the water and toothpaste is detrimental to health, shuts down our pineal gland, which is the gland that raises our consciousness.

7 – FERTILIZER AND PESTICIDES

The World Economic Forum through their control of Governments around the world are interfering with world wide access to fertilisers, insisting that fertiliser use is reduced, by 95 percent.
The war in Ukraine has affected the production, supply and export of fertilizer.

Pesticides manufactured by Monsanto were attacked in the USA Supreme Court. The Company and Liability were offloaded and sold to a German chemical company Beyer. The product is still being manufactured in a friendlier manufacturing environment, and causing harm to the insects, bees and wildlife around the world, except the USA.

School meals in America have glyphosate and heavy metals present in ninety percent of the meals tested. The poisons levels measured in the children's bodies are considered dangerous.

8 – FARMING INDUSTRY

The farmers in Holland are openly rebelling against their government's policy which has reduced fertiliser use by ninety-five percent, and escalated the price.

Dutch farmers are the most productive in the world. The Dutch government has a budget of EU $28 billion of taxpayer money to purchase the forced bankruptcy of farmers' properties, and turn these areas into wilding, or housing schemes for the Elites. Modern day pirate's at work, stealing from the farmers, and in reducing the food grown, the added benefit of starving the population.

German, Austrian, Czechia Republic, Italian and French farmers are joining the Dutch farmers protest, as the various Governments' Policy is rolled out like an ever expanding lava field after a volcano.

The price of fertiliser has increased by 250 percent. The price of seeds has doubled. Farming costs have risen by 300 percent, with future major supply problems in store, as farms cannot afford to grow, because of cost restraints.

The only way forward is to reduce acreage planted to operate with escalating costs. What price will the consumer have to pay, food riots, diminished supply, extremely high unaffordable prices.

All the governments are singing from the same hymn sheet, have been compromised, the World Economic Forum plan to bankrupt the small farmer, and establish industrialised farming, or destroy farming, and starve the people is playing out.

Perhaps it is time for the Amish farming methods to be extended worldwide, where horses are used for ploughing the land. That said, the FBI in America are attacking the independent Amish farmers to put them out of business.

9 – GLOBAL FOOD SUPPLIES

In America, more than one hundred companies have mysteriously had fires destroying their ability to produce food. These companies presumably do not fit into the World Economic Forum sphere of control, and are condemned, with a World Economic Forum Company benefitting from the vacuum created by escalating production in Cabal financed companies.

Baby milk factories have been closed.

Nestle milk powder selling scams.

New mothers are given free samples, sufficient to dry up a mother's milk. This is trapping her into buying dried milk, mixed with flour, degrading the nourishment value. In poor countries, it results in a much higher death rate among the children.

In Ethiopia, the Government nationalised the food companies, to control prices, during a time of high prices. Once prices stabilised, a decision was then made to sell the companies. Nestle bought one, and promptly sued for six million US dollars during a drought and famine.
They are steeply entrenched in Lawfare.

Nestle Purina brands are not a healthy option for a healthy dog. The sachets have a 25 year shelf life, and the law as it stands will support Nestle in a legal action against them if your pet's death can be linked to the Purina foods. No financial compensation is given for the loss of a pet.

Nestle uses forced labour as young as eight years old in the third world. They grow cocoa, the workers beaten to improve productivity. In many cases, these children are carrying up to twice their weight in cocoa.

Bird flu has been introduced into the chicken industry causing the destruction of millions of poultry farms, eggs and chickens, and turkeys. Cattle in Texas, 10,000 died mysteriously, the heat being blamed.

Impossible food burgers is a genetically modified yeast “plant” product modified soya protein. The SLH gives it the taste, but it is poisonous. Tested on rats, which resulted in the development of multiple organ toxicity, changes in weight, blood, anaemia, and sterility were recorded.

Rat tests were only conducted over 28 days. Results suggest herbicides in the food.

Beyond meat burgers has a much higher level of toxicity and has been withdrawn by many food outlets in the USA. Amazingly Approved by the F.D.A. – Food and Drug Administration.

FDA is financed by the food industry. FDA management is an approval authority to approve corruption. Industry representatives, in a revolving door, are seconded to run the FDA, and return to Industry after the introduction of their desired legislation is approved.

In the USA, the public schools 90% of the meals have dangerous levels of glyphosate, weed killer, herbicides and heavy metals in the meals. The result is sterilisation of the children, a future bomb yet to explode on humanity. Graphene, a liquid metal and poisonous to humans, interferes with the body's electrical system and is used in food.

Food supply lines are disrupted, internationally causing shortages, and famines worldwide, especially in poor countries, with a huge loss of life through starvation.
Four international food corporation control ninety percent of the world food production.

No doubt, a promise has been made to hand over 3,000 Dutch farmer's properties to the International Corporations to further monopolise world food production.

B12 is a synthetic light metal, hydrogen cyanide. Something as simple as B12 vitamin tablets contain cyanocobalamin. Cobalt metal is dropped into the body molecule; the cyanide steals oxygen from the body, which is not declared to the consumer.

The changes in the human DNA from 3d, to 4d and 5d requires mankind to adapt the body to clean organic food, superfoods, fruit and vegetarian lifestyle, cutting out sugar and bread to obtain the maximum improvement in mental and physical benefits.

It is only fair to give Klaus Schwab, Founder and Chairman of the World Economic Forum and Author of the Book "Covid-19: The Great Reset" the right of reply:

"At least 4 billion "useless eaters" shall be eliminated by the year 2050 by means of fatal rapid acting diseases, and starvation.

Energy, food and water shall be kept at subsistence levels for the non-elites, starting with the White population of Western Europe and North America and then spreading to other races.

The population of Canada, Western Europe and United States will be decimated more rapidly than the other continents, until the world's population reaches a manageable level of 1 billion, of which 500 million will consist of Chinese and Japanese races, selected because they are people who have been regimented for centuries and who are accustomed to obeying authority without question.

From the time there shall be artificially contrived food and water shortages and medical care to remind the masses that their very existence depends on the goodwill of the Committee of 300."

An excerpt from his book in four sentences.

10 – BIG PHARMA

Pfizer paid US $2,875,842 bribe to the FDA, through the US Treasury, a bribe for their mRNA Bioweapon approval. The payment to the Treasury breaks the link between Pfizer and the FDA directly.

Pfizer, Moderna, Johnson & Johnson, are the main USA suppliers of mRNA vaccines. Much is now coming out against these vaccines and the damage they do. These corporations have sold their souls to Satan, sold their vaccines to governments in legal contracts that have absolved them from financial assault. Governments have legally absolved them of malfeasance in their product. Pfizer's test results were based on experimenting on eight mice.

The Pfizer vaccine was never tested to see whether it stopped transmission of the virus. Governments issued COVID passports, stopped outdoor activities, crushing businesses, cost jobs amongst many. A high level conspiracy, by copying, the actions which were taking place in China. The outbreak started in China in 2019.

Tucker Carlson interviewed the UK's Doctor Aseem Malhotra on corruption of medicine by Big Pharma. Dr Malhotra is from Manchester, and trained in Edinburgh. He practices in London and specialises in heart diseases, and surgery. His father, aged 73, died unexpectedly after the Pfizer mRNA vaccine, and a full post mortem was carried out. Vested interests have corrupted the medical profession's yellow card information reporting on unexplained side effects and deaths from medicines.

Pathologist, Dr Ryan Cole, warns of foot long blood clots being found in autopsies of post mRNA patients in a discussion with Dr Kelly Victory, and Dr Drew.

In the N.H.S., more patients are coming forward with more serious conditions, with heart disease. Flawed science is allowed to stand – statins are prescribed to 1 billion people, data industry sponsored by Big Pharma, and the Medical Profession, but statins only help 1% of the patients taking them, the other 99% do not benefit.
Big Pharma are misleading the Medical Profession, and the general public taking them.

Statins interfere with the quality of life. Proposed lifestyle changes, and exercise are more beneficial.

Evidence based medicine is an illusion, as it has been hijacked by Big Pharma paying Doctors for opinions which influenced the correct outcome.

Heart attacks induced by COVID-19, Pfizer mRNA vaccines. Imaging of the heart facts relating to mRNA vaccine are being withheld, because the

Medical Industry do not wish to lose funding from Big Pharma.

Regulations have been influenced by Big Pharma, and have lost their objectivity.

The shutdowns imposed by Governments had no value, except impose control over the population, and seriously impact human rights.

The human gene has a spiral coil which has two strands. Each strand has 72,000 genes for the father, and 72,000 genes for the mother. Total of 144,000 genes. If a third strand is added through the mRNA vaccine, the total would be 216,000 genes.

216,000 genes equals 600 x 60 x 6 = 666 in GEMATRIA. The mark of the BEAST: SATAN.

The USA illegal government has purchased US $300 million in anti-radiation sickness drugs, bought by HHS, suggesting that there is a plan for a nuclear war.

CDC – Centre for Disease Control is financed by the Big Pharma Industry. CDC Management is an

Approval Authority for Big Pharma's Approved Corruption.

Industry representatives are seconded to run the CDC, in a revolving door policy, and return to industry, after the introduction of their desired legislation is approved.

An appeal has been made to the police in the UK to confiscate all Pfizer and Moderna vaccines, as they are dangerous to life. Evidence provided.

The USA Government has confirmed that COVID Vaccination caused a 1433x increase in reports of Cancer to the CDC Database.

Gilead, a Big Pharma corporation invented a cure for illness in weeks. Goldman Sacs refused to finance this drug, on the grounds that Gilead would go bankrupt due to curing the illness prior to their ability to service the debt.

This demonstrates that Big Pharma is not working on behalf of the sick, and the Medical Profession is complicit in the fraud.

BLOOD TRANSFUSION DONATIONS WORLD WIDE.

We donate, Big Pharma exploit. Did you sign an informed consent form?

There are 100 million donations made worldwide. Twenty percent is for hospital use. Eighty percent is sold to private companies to exploit the market for blood products. It is a commodity that is more expensive than oil. Three companies control the market worldwide, C.S.L., GRIFOL, and OCTOPHARMA

Sales by Octopharma alone are worth US $1.5 billion per year. Plasma cannot be exported, but drugs can. Plasma is used to extract proteins, ten percent of the blood plasma trade. The owner of Octopharma is worth US $6 billion, and the company is worth US $17 billion – family owned.
In America, donations of blood are worth US $200 per month providing you are able to make two donations every week. Payment is made to a cash card. The poor exploit this to survive. Very little is done to ensure the donor is fit enough to make the donation.

It is exploited by drug addicts to pay for their drugs. Unfortunately, the next step is the card is taken away from the addict by the dealer to ensure payment. The dealer provides a transport service to the addict, returns the card whilst the donor gives his blood, then the dealer removes the card to pay for the drugs. Repeat, repeat.

It is also used by moneylenders to secure payment of a loan to the poor.

Plasma origin is kept secret, remember the scandal in the NHS hospitals HIV infected blood enquiry ongoing for fifty years after scandal broke.

America controls seventy five percent of the world market, and the FDA administers and controls the market.
Long term health issues in the poor are not studied. It is known tiredness, headaches, lack of energy, and blackouts are common.

BRITAINS NATIONAL HEALTH SERVICE HAS BEEN WEAPONISED.

The Secretary of State for Health and Social Care automatically becomes the sole shareholder of

Genomics England. The object is to obtain the DNA of the Patients of the NHS. A clear conflict of interest exists between the people of Britain and Genomics England. Major privacy laws and issues are being broken.

Genomics Ltd, (UK) is part of a worldwide corporation, and Genomics England is probably a subsidiary. Since Matthew John David Hancock was Health Secretary, it would not surprise me if he is also a shareholder in Genomics (UK). He has retired from Government, and the new explosive growth industry to invest in is Euthanasia, introduced by the World Economic Forum as Policy.

The Westminster Government in the pocket of the World Economic Forum and BIG PHARMA, have passed Legislation NICE NG163 of 3rd April 2020. This is superseded by NICE NG191 of 14th July 2022, which sets out the "END OF LIFE PATHWAY PROTOCOL."

NICE began as a negative term derived from the Latin word; "nescius", meaning in English "stupid, unaware, ignorant, foolish person". It was borrowed from the French in the 1300s, the meaning has returned to its original roots.

The National Institute for Care and Excellence or NICE are trying to fool us with their end of life pathway protocol.

A contract has been placed with an as yet unidentified company to supply various drugs to the NHS to speed up the NHS's patient's departure from the NHS Care in this world.

This is fronted by a relatively new company with BIG PHARMA providing the drugs required without being directly named as suppliers. Lots of practise obtained during the COVID-19 virus outbreak.

This new company will provide fifty two percent of the lethal drugs required by the NHS.

Jeremy Hunt as Chancellor has just approved all the elderly and disabled will have £100K taken from their estate to pay for their end of life care.

There is a population planned euthanasia point system to hasten death. In England, 1,642 are planned to be murdered by doctors and nurses every day. Reported to be 370,814 thousand annually, increasing to 448,507 thousand annually by 2031.

The above figures do not add up, 365 days x 1642 daily equals 599,330 victims annually. This is being achieved by the use of a combination of drugs, using lorazipam, remdesivir, diazepam, opiods, and midazolam.

During COVID-19 it was known that drugs were being overprescribed. Doctors will be financially incentivised to act. £9,000 per day to motivate doctors and nurses.

That enables BIG PHARMA to stand proud and declare: "It Wisna Me." We did not know what the drugs were being used for.

I hope the First Minister of Scotland trials it on herself to see if it works before she inflicts it on the Scottish People.

DAVID ROCKERFELLER SPEECH 1991 made it clear that he sought complete control of the world. He thanked the Washington Post, and other newspapers representatives for maintaining secrecy, and not declaring the content of the discussions.

KISSINGER SPEECH FEBRUARY 2009

Quote to the W.H.O. Council on Eugenics:

"Once the herd accepts mandatory vaccinations, its game over. They will accept anything – forcible blood or organ donation……For the greater good". "Control sheep minds and you control the herd. Vaccine makers stand to make billions, and many of you in this room are investors. It is a win, win. We thin out the herd, and the herd pays us for extermination services!"

It is obvious who MATTHEW JOHN DAVID HANCOCK, AND JEREMY HUNT REPRESENT. IT IS NOT THE BRITISH PEOPLE.

11 – TRANSPORTATION SYSTEM TRUCKS, TRAINS, AND PLANES.

Highway transportation disrupted by legislation in California. 70,000 trucks have been banished from California roads because of the new environmental laws.

Railways disrupted by derailments, sabotage and labour strikes. Diesel fuel in short supply.

The air transportation industry is being destroyed by carbon credit charges. It should be kept in mind that the world's elites 1% of the population charter market equals 50% of the world air travel by the other 99% of the world's air transport travellers.

It seems to me imperative that the Global Air Charter Flights should immediately be shut down to save the planet, and allow the deplorables to fly undisturbed by the elites.

Sea shipping has collapsed, manufacturing has collapsed, empty ships! Many empty ships are being scrapped, so the future of ship transport is severely curtailed.

There is a bright side to this picture; the West's sanctions placed on Russian Oil and Gas has resulted in Russia buying up all the Oil Tankers for sale to transport their oil around the world. The world price of second hand tankers has doubled through Russia's desire to increase its fleet.

Transportation has been disrupted by restricted fuel supply and driving hours, high fuel costs increasing 100%, and the reduction in world supplies of oil and gas.

12 – FORESTRY MARKET

Illegal forestry is allowed to happen in the USA and elsewhere by creating forest fires. This allowed permission to log the forest after the fires.
Premeditated fires and logging in National Parks, only by an approved mafia contractor.

13 – MINING MARKET

Through the illuminati controlled companies, large shareholdings were purchased allowing the complete control of price and supply.

14 – SPORTS INDUSTRY

The sports spectacles of Olympics, FIFA World Cup Football, Rugby, swimming, Commonwealth Games were glamorised, and extravagant parades took place heavily influenced by Satanic Design, intent and ceremony.

15 – HOLLYWOOD

Hollywood are deeply controlled by the Illuminati, they are a key corrupt propaganda machine for the World Economic Forum.

The Hollywood Film Industry was financed by Centurion Global Fund, a Vatican subsidiary. They financed the film "Rocket Man," the story of Elton John.

Disney is now a failing company, and is not expected to survive, much bad news still has to be revealed.

16 – UNCONTROLLED IMMIGRATION

Illuminati planned and financed the uncontrolled smuggling of fentanyl drugs, and also import 100 million people into America, after which there relatives will be invited into America. Lara Logan of Real American Voice was firm on the 100 million people.

Ukrainians, and other economic migrants, and refugees are being sucked into Europe and the UK with the aim to create humanity 3.0!

17 – MAINSTREAM MEDIA AND SOCIAL MEDIA.

THE Rothschild's bought Reuters Central News Agency and the Associated Press in the 1800's to be able to influence the news.

Through the early years of the Rothschild's, Rockefeller's, Oppenheimer Brotherhood, and the J.P. Morgan money cartels sought to buy a controlling interest in the biggest newspapers. This is to ensure the interests of the group were represented by the newspapers, and their secret interests were defined, and protected from scrutiny.

In 1917 J.P Morgan formed a FRONT GROUP –

THE COUNCIL OF FOREIGN RELATIONS

Their headquarters is in New York City, and stated objective:

"To create a world system of financial control in private hands; able to dominate the political system of each country; and the economy of the world as a whole."

Their policy, after research, was to purchase the rights to control the newspapers content, and political agenda.
It was found that they needed to get control in the beginning of twelve newspapers around America.
In short, they seek complete control of the entire world.

Senator Oscar Calloway was so concerned he reported the matter to Congress.

The plan to control was simple; they bought a controlling interest in the newspaper, and appointed the Managing Editor; in each newspaper, thus controlling the flow of information to the readers.

Today, that number has been expanded, and also includes all the major TV and Radio news stations, cinemas, and public entertainment. Newscorp, Viacom, Disney, Facebook and Twitter are other company examples.

Certain companies like General Electric, Westinghouse, Raetheon, Grumman, promote their interest in war activities.

Much of the newspaper income comes from advertising, and this too was obtained through the cartels instructions to companies they had an interest in.

This gave the financial cartel an ability to persuade the big corporations to advertise and also Government Approved Corporate Sponsorship of TV shows and Sports events.

This had the ability to divert the attention of the people away from the important issues happening in the world of the day, today!

Much effort also goes into keeping the Public in a State of Fear, with exaggerated stories, outright lies, and many of pure fiction, whilst two thirds of the world population go hungry.

All the companies are under the control of criminal minds, CNN is in financial trouble because the Public are no longer being taken in by the deception.
MSM, CNN is being sued by Donald Trump for US $475 million for defamation of character, after which all other corrupt MSM outlets will be sued by Trump.
Elon Musk has bought Twitter, and has exposed more than 50% algorithm generated responses. Adverting revenue has shrunk, but major truth is being brought to light, and will expose many deceitful beings.

Facebook is also being exposed, their share value collapsed, and Zuckerberg changed its name to META, which in Hebrew means "DEATH."

Both Facebook and Twitter were involved in funding and supporting the election fraud. Legal proceedings have not been upheld at this time.

The barriers of illusion are being removed by the Internet Freedom Fraternity, and their Truth Tellers.

In the early 1960s, a book favourable to the Council of Foreign Relations was written by Professor Caroll Quigly, who was given privileged access to their records to create an influence pedalling book to sell their services.

In 2022, Justin Trudeau legislated against streaming companies with the addition of C11 Online Streaming Act.
Section 9.1: The Commission may in furtherance of the objects make orders imposing conditions on the carrying on of broadcasting, undertakings, that the Commission considers appropriate for the implementation of the broadcasting policy set out in subsection 3.1 including conditions respecting ...
Section 9.1 (1)e: The presentation of programmes and services for selection by the public, including the show casing and discountability of Canadian Programs and Programming Services, such as original French Language
Programs.

Canadian Government has given themselves the power to control news, input and output.

Rebel News Canada is under threat for reporting truth. They won a Court Judgement against the Government, which enabled them to lift a ban on their representatives attending Government News Briefs. They are, however, banned from asking questions.

The bail out money freely given by the Canadian Government supports the subservient media.
The above reality is to attack Canada's citizen's rights, and freedom of expression.
The mainstream media and social media have become the lapdogs of government, and elites, and the watchdog on the deplorable, but there is a glimmer of hope. Twitter, through Elon Musk's intervention, has become a Whistle-blower on the Representatives of Corruption. Freedom of Speech is fighting back to awaken humanity.

As Davos rises on the horizon for its annual publicity campaign, the voices of the WEF have cancelled Elon Musk and Twitter, and are now recommending all listeners to join the Chinese TickTok Internet Company for their news.

18 – REPUBLICS REPLACING WORLD ROYALTY

The monopolies created over thousands of years are being broken up. An equalisation of the law, providing sovereign law is adopted removes the privilege of Royals who never have enough.

Smaller single party governments without lobbyists need to be introduced, and power devolved downwards to the local communities.

19 – LAWFARE

False and never-ending law suits are used to silence the opposition using the tax payer's money, against a tax payer. Mainstream media are used, to endlessly attack truth-speakers. The voices of reason are shouted down by the black hat spoilers. Few cases have ever been won by anyone fighting, suing a Bank through the Courts.
Banks have stolen billions.

California has introduced 5 new laws on the 1st of January 2023.

SB 107: “Sanctuary State” for “Transgender Kids” protects the right of the child to use drugs, or surgery to provide “gender affirming care” to any child within the USA.
AB 2098: “COVID Misinformation” seeks through their medical licencing board to punish doctors with an opinion that does not accord with the States opinion.
AB 2147: Decriminalizing Jaywalking Because of Racism. “Freedom to Walk Act”
SB 1375: Allowing Nurses to Perform Abortions Without Doctors.
SB 357: Decriminalizing Loitering for Prostitution.
On Hold: AB 257 State Control of Fast Food Restaurants. Council empowered to set wages and working conditions in the industry. Law suspended until a referendum held.
SB 1327: Allowing Private Citizens to Sue for Gun Violations.

A Polish/American doctor, Dr Burzynski, has a 100% cure for cancer that is very effective, developed in the 1980s, and the Texas State Federal Government, and the FDA have involved him in spurious Law cases at the highest level – six grand juries. They have confiscated his patients’ medical records which took him twelve years to recover. He was pursued for 14 years through the Courts and F.D.A., and Dr Burzynski's Medical Patents were stolen, by duplication.

The Federal Government in Washington DC threatened him with a US $18.5 Million fine, and 290 years in jail.

There is an extremely malignant cancer in the legal minds of these people that pursue the destruction of good medicine. The cost to the Taxpayer was US $62 Million, yes US $62 million! And to Dr Burzynski, US $2.2 Million. Why? They were stealing his PATENTS. First do no harm?

20 – LAW OF NESARA/GESARA

On September 15th, 2012 the Tribunal Court of the People Natural and Common Law was established in Brussels.

Currently, all Attorneys at the Bar are "Esquires" as nobles under the will of the King, and the Bank of England "Esquire" is a title of nobility.

Every corporate, government, evil entity, and banking system has been cancelled, in place fully effective on 1st January, 2023.

The crimes of the Duke and Queen Elizabeth 11 are in partnership with the VATICAN POPE. The crimes under review are against the indigenous peoples of Canada.

All lawyers have to retrain.

21 – WHISTLEBLOWERS.

This is the place that it is most appropriate to introduce WikiLeaks, their massive flooding of the internet with truthful information, files of the elites, governments, and deep state actions, which exposed their crimes to humanity.
It was planned by a positive A.I., which released the information in 2010. Sadly, this has resulted in a paranoid pursuit of Julian Assange since 2010, and his life has been one of a refugee, and prisoner of the corrupt legal system ever since, in the corrupt world governments' and elites' attempts to protect their secrets from disclosure.

Many people are coming forward to tell the truth and expose the lies, undermining the mainstream media.

22 – BITCOIN BLOCKCHAIN, A SIGN OF INSECURITY

Electronic internet of E Cash. Satoshi believed to hold one million bitcoin. Satoshi Nakamoto registered bitcoin in August 2008 – Digital money. First valuation was US $0.00008 cents. By month end, this was US $0.08 cents. First transaction was 10 bitcoin on 3rd January, 2009, loss of faith in fiat money. First purchase was two pizzas for 10,000 bitcoin.

Ten bitcoin were sold, and by 2013, each bitcoin was US$100.00, rest is history.

The Winklevoss twins 6'5" tall made US $500 million out of Facebook. They became angel investors. Facebook restricted their ability to trade. Facebook used Lawfare to enforce it, so they moved to Ibiza in 2011.

They met Azar, and Charlie Shrem and invested in Exchange Mt. Gox selling. Bitcoin sales were 1 million a month increasing to 30 million.

Bitcoin was used by the Silk Road, the most illegal business in the world. Charlie Shrem as CEO was arrested and sent to Jail for two years for laundering money for the Silk Road, without reporting to the F.B.I.

The company Mt. Gox went bankrupt, and the Winklevoss twins opened up the Gemeni Exchange in 2014 to continue the business, making them both billionaires.

I believe the C.I.A. are heavily involved in bitcoin to hide their illegal payments. Bitcoin is a database used by speculators, and all monies will be stolen. It is a massive Ponzi scheme and Satoshi does not exist.

FTX has just gone bankrupt, never had a board meeting yet valued at US $32 billion. They did not know how much money they had. US $16 billion is missing. The man in charge, Sam Bankman-Fried, did not know how many employees he had and had a US $1 billion personal loan, and funded the Democratic Party Election. Biden has been asked to return the money.

John Ray 111 who sorted out the Enron Bankruptcy at its collapse stated that FTX was a chaotic fraudulent mess, complete failure of corporate controls, and absence of trustworthy financial information.

23 – SATANIC RITUALS

Location of Satanic Temples?

Vatican, Buckingham Palace, Washington DC White House, and Epstein Island. Many others are still not exposed. How many child sacrifices were made over the years?

Recent Gematria dates
2022: July 8th Shinzo Abe Assassinated
Aug 8th Mar a Lago Raided

2022: Sept 8th: Queen Elizabeth 11 dies.
: Oct 8th: Crimean bridge attack.
: Nov 8th: mid-term elections.
: Dec 8th: ?

24 – CHILD AND SEX TRAFFICKING

UNICEF, USAID, Save the Children are all used to traffic children. They simply disappear at a convenient location into a d.u.m.b. It is thought millions of children were trafficked around the world annually. 700,000 children disappeared from Haiti after hurricane Matthew.

Chelsea Clinton and her husband were found guilty in a Military Tribunal of child kidnap. I do not know if the death sentence has been carried out on them at Guantanamo Bay in Cuba.

Jimmy Saville was a very good friend of King Charles 111.
It is reported that four Christian Charities are involved in this evil trade.

25 – ADRENACHROME MANUFACTURE AND ORGAN TRAFFICKING

Adrenochrome is a chemical compound produced by the oxidation of adrenaline. It was linked as a potential cause of schizophrenia, but that theory has been discounted.

Adrenachrome is a drug one hundred times stronger than heroin, developed from the blood of children. It is a massive industry, and only survives by the death of a child. Similarly, organ transplant survives on the back of sacrifice.

Another drug which is possible is Acromochrome, which is manufactured from the bodies of the dead.

Google it would appear has blocked access to online sites with analysis and information.

26 – FENTANYL

A very potent synthetic opioid, used for pain medication.
Manufactured in China and smuggled around the world.
Drug addicts use it worldwide.

27 – DISNEYWORLD AND THE CHILD TRAFFICKING INDUSTRY

First do no harm.
Walt Disney was a heavy smoker of Lucky Strike, and his daughter was concerned. She asked Walt to use a cigarette holder and filter – the filter medium was asbestos. He went into hospital on the 2nd of

November, 1966, for his lung to be removed. Six weeks later, he died in hospital on the 15th of December, 1966.

Big Tobacco, Big Pharma, and the Medical Profession involved in his death at 65.

Walt had a flat in the castle of the Magic Kingdom, Why I wonder?

Disneyworld in Florida had the same Tax Status as Washington DC. Disneyworld had its own Police Force not answerable to anyone else. This has been withdrawn by the Florida Governor Ron De Santis, ensuring that Disneyworld is policed, and pays its taxes like everyone else.

There is a submarine tunnel into Disneyworld from the Atlantic to traffic children. This was all part of the Epstein and Ghislaine Maxwell sphere of operations.

28 – EDUCATION

Transgenderism seeks to divide society, and generate hate. Wokeism is the word being used to divide family through the education system. It is grooming the children.

Teachers are encouraged to interfere in a child's sexuality and sow doubt in the mind of the child. Thus, by such means encourage the children to take puberty blockers, which are known to cause infertility in teenagers. Knowing the agenda to reduce the world population to 500 million, by any means necessary, it meets the NEW WORLD ORDER'S objective.

Wokeism must be removed from the worldwide education curriculum. Woke teachers too need to be removed from teaching, certainly re-educated.

The new transgender LBGTQ+ books in school libraries make Lady Chatterley look like a children's comic. These books are explicit and obscene. Parents need to take back control of the school. Parental panels must instruct clear guidelines to the teachers, who are putting children at risk, and make a clear statement to limit teaching responsibility.

UK's armed forces are required to employ 60% man and 40% man with a womb, as the politically correct LBGTQ+ have removed woman from the dictionary.

This is not good, as the training they receive can never, by the law of averages, match a man.

Legislation may not have caught up with the woke thinking to insist on a 50/50% man/man with a womb in the workplace, perhaps that should be woke place!

Certain industries training may mean you have a labour force of trained males of 100,000, and man with a womb only 5,000. The Law requires that the 5,000 are employed but their experience and strength may not be suitable, or comparable to the 100,000 males.

Similarly minorities must be included, and if the staff has to be made redundant, the priority is to fire the white employees.

There is a planned street protest in Edinburgh to highlight objections to wokism outside the Scottish Assembly Building on the 12th January 2023 at 11.30am.

29 – WORLD POLITICS, PROXY WARS, & MILITARY FORCES

Russia is being demonised by the USA, UK and EU

The Ukraine uprising in 2014 against the Government was financed and controlled by the USA/Illuminati to turn Ukraine into a centre for money laundering, child and sex trafficking, drug trafficking, adrenachrome manufacturing, and 46 bio labs producing viruses on an industrial scale to spring upon an unsuspecting world.

It was imperative that Russia moved before the release of these viruses, which would have provided the successor to COVID-19, and brought disaster to the Ukrainian people and Russia first. There is evidence through body language and football that Putin and Trump are working together to expose all these traitors.

High on the list is Biden's son, with his business interests in Ukraine.

Ukraine States of Luhansk, Donetsk, Kherson, and

Zaporizhzhia have been holding state wide voting on a referendum to join Russia. They were ceded to Russia on 1st October, 2022, after eight years of genocide and military attacks by the Nazi Regiments of Ukraine, on the mainly Russian population.

The current proxy war between USA/Ukraine against Russia will probably bring down the illuminati, and their supporters worldwide. It is also collapsing the American Dollar.

The armed forces of the world are at the beck and call of their Governments which are controlled by External non- government forces, and massive corporate greed by the companies wishing to benefit from war.

Mike Lindell has stated that President Bolsonaro of Brazil has had 5.1 million votes stolen from him through the voting machines. Bolsonaro recently had a meeting with Trump.

The DECLARATION OF NORTH AMERICA (DNA) was signed on the 10th January 2023 by Biden, Trudeau, and President Andreas Manuel Lopez Obrador, which is an agreement to combine the countries of Canada, America and Mexico.

30 – CLIMATE LOCKDOWN

THE W.E.F. has a plan to introduce climate lockdowns on the Sabbath affecting church attendance, by preventing private transport use to save the planet. This has been introduced in various ways around the globe.

31 – REMEDIAL ACTIONS

A Global Communications blackout must happen to dismantle the old Swift banking system, and introduce the new global Nesara/Gesara system. It is hack proof, and it will not take long to arrive. We await the collapse of the US $, UK £, and EU Euro.

This may not be true because the Christmas, New Year Holidays permitted the time required.

Elon Musk's Starlink will introduce satellite communications, and it is rumoured 6 billion Q phones will be required to replace current phones, for financial transactions. They are hack proof phones.

Notwithstanding the above, there has to be a major task throughout the world to arrest, try and imprison the traitors and criminals running this world wide cabal.

32 – GLOBAL GOVERNMENTS

Governments are using our taxes to engineer our demise, and seize power. Governments need Big Tech databases to spy on everybody. Drug trade controls Government money transfers in the shadows, and infiltrating mob activities undetected by Law Enforcement. Crime families pay no taxes, and operate in the black economy.
Dominion voting machines control world elections. Voting results are weaponised, and fraudulent. Big Tech and Big Pharma are militarised, Tactical disinformation in play, to maintain the fog of war. Cabal own and control the railways in the USA.

The reality is governments have now been overwhelmed by the demands of the Worlds Global Companies, over 100 have already introduced Environmental Social Governance (E.S.G.) Scores for their staff, and hiring new employee based on these criteria. This is linked to the United Nations Sustainable Goals, which actually achieve the opposite to that which is claimed. More companies are signing up as the power play benefit is realised by these companies not yet signed up.

That also works in the opposite direction placing pressure on the farmers, and others to comply with the Sustainable Rules created for that market. The NEW CONTROLLERS are not Government and not the voter.

Voters elect Government Members, who then represent themselves in power. These individuals in the majority have become professional criminals and fraudsters, representing the agenda of the World Economic Forum.

They pretend in their Government Assemblies to represent opposing parties, who do not agree. The reality is, behind the curtain, they are planning the fraud on the people. These individuals prepare the Acts of Parliament in accordance with the World Economic Forum Plans, and formulate the language to deceive the real intent behind the funding, to maintain the W.E.F secrecy.

By the time funds are distributed by trusty staff, the Parliamentary time is being used on other matters, and no close scrutiny is made on how the money is actually spent. The W.E.F. Parliamentary representatives are rewarded in various ways, behind the huge cloak of Commercial Corporations.

ITALY

The Vatican was raided, popes, arch bishops arrested, and the riches beneath the Vatican confiscated.

Baby factory, depressed and restrained women used to produce babies. Adrenachrome manufacturing now stopped. Human child trafficking was a problem.

Elites cleaned out.

A movie was produced called “Sound of Freedom”

SPAIN

Spain sold out to the Deep State in 2016. Male trafficking is a problem, being cleaned out. Whistle-blowers are coming forward.

FRANCE

Women are being held in baby factories. Young boys are being used by the Dark Cult. Clean up operations extensive. Clearing out this repulsive industry will take time. White Hat soldiers 200 in number died in operations to destroy this ongoing trade. The enemy has well equipped adversaries to overwhelm. Much remains to be done.

GREECE

Greece is a hotbed of D.U.M.B.s and the party culture. Kidnapping is more open and above ground. The Governments and Elites agree to support the new regime, but not trusted to keep agreement.
Off-Worlders are coming to Greece, portal for their landing. Deep State has not kept agreement, therefore, have been cleaned out.

33 – GLOBAL BANKING INDUSTRY

Planned inflation will cause escalation in the price of goods. Interest rates will be increased above the inflation rate to defeat the inflation, collapsing property prices will result.

Escalating interest rates will disrupt, or bankrupt the mortgage market and industry.

Repossessions will enrich the Banks.

34 – GLOBAL STOCK MARKETS

A steady, and on occasions, rapid collapse of stock prices will happen, especially after a currency collapse when mass panic rules supreme.

35 – DOWNFALL OF THE EVIL CABAL

I believe in heaven, there are the AKASHIC RECORDS.
These are the word of GOD, recording everyone's actions and behaviour monitored by your Guardian Angels, and GOD's Warrior Angels.

Much of what men do is recorded in advance of their actions over their lifetime, this enables GOD to keep ahead of Satan's actions, and enables GOD's Prophecies to be accurate.

We are entering a modern day Exodus of Egypt, but on a much larger scale to encompass the earth.

GOD is dismantling the planned One World Government, the Pharaoh of today.

Vengeance is GOD's, not mans. GOD will remove Satan and his servants in a day. Righteous rebellion is inspiring GOD's people.

The Cabal is finished, but we have to defeat the negative A.I., which has no soul and no link to GOD.

SECRETS OF THE UNIVERSE

THE SOUND OF MUSIC

In my mind, nothing compares to Boogie Woogie for energy, vibrancy, and taking years off your life.

Much was handed down by word of mouth over the millennia regarding music and its positive and negative energies.

Nicola Tesla had considerable knowledge of energy, frequency, vibration, and sound. This has considerable health benefits if utilised in the correct way.

Thus, the opposite of the above, has a very negative force field too, and this has been exploited by mean spirited humans for their own purposes.

The Rockefeller Foundation took control of music in 1939, and established the 440Hz standard tuning fork, which has a strong influence on recorded music today.
All music is legally obliged to use the 440Hz as a base standard tuning, which precisely established the F Sharp note, 741Hz.

The negative forces plans were to shut down the human brain to control it, with negative, destructive behaviour. This raises mental health issues, and undermines our direct relationship with GOD.

When driving a car, the farther away you get from the radio signal, it diminishes the signal to a static level. This is designed to frustrate, anger, and accepting static as music!

93% of the function of human DNA is light, sound reception and transmission; photon, phonon reception, transmission for intercellular communication, and cellular upregulation, meaning precipitation in the now, present, every millisecond, your re-manifesting in water. Water is the most energy conductive of all materials in the human body, a super conductor. Your DNA is an energy amplifier using 3, 6 and 9, Tesla's Vortex numbers.

Human DNA is a hard drive memory and antenna to our Creator GOD, and His Son, Jesus Christ.

The earth has a magnetic field around it, with a North and South Pole. The human body also has a magnetic field surrounding it, with the head being North, and the feet being the South Pole. Could it be the other way round?
The planet has 9 core creative notes, 396, 417, 528, 639, 741, and 852Hz, the first 6 are registered on the Solfeggio scale, and frequencies.

8 Hz is the frequency of the earth.

110 Hz - If the sound vibration frequency is set to this frequency then the human body can feel it.

Many ancient structures reflect the above sound qualities off the walls. In Ireland, Malta, and elsewhere, this has been demonstrated. It provides the subject with an out of body experience at 110Hz. (to tap into our minds?)

154.7Hz – Zero point Void Meditation Frequency

417Hz – clears away all negative energy and blockages.

The Schumann Resonance: The Soul Vibrates.
432 Hz: Magic Frequency to attract miracles.

(Not used, forbidden in mainstream media music)

With the right frequency, two objects resonating at the same vibration can transmit energy to each other.
Perfect example of that is a tuning fork at 440Hz used in music.

440Hz to 440Hz Energy transmitted between two or more forks, 30 feet apart, give off the same sound vibration.
440Hz to 442Hz Energy is not transmitted.

The 440Hz frequency has been scientifically proved to be detrimental to your DNA, and is used by Radio, TV, and Cinema, at this level, to weaken the human race.

444Hz an angel frequency, it increases brain function, and reduces stress levels. It improves your sleep.

528Hz: Love wavelength, DNA healing and repair.
This frequency is almost the precise centre of the electro-magnetic colour spectrum, which is the same as the sound spectrum. Massive evidence

that 528Hz planet is in dissonance with another note or frequency.
586 Hz
594 Hz
666 Hz: Angelic Frequency – Pure Light.
741 Hz: Devils Interval:
What is known as the “Devil’s Interval” is music on the528Hz Range, coupled with 741 Hz range, which creates an annoying noise, affecting the health of the individual, possibly resulting in death.

777Hz: Attract Positivity, Luck and Abundance.

852Hz: Frequency helps to replace negative thoughts with positive ones in the mind, making it ideal for nervous or anxious people.

888Hz: Frequency, what we put out into the world will come back to us. Known as the angelic frequency.

963 Hz: Frequency of the GODS

999Hz: Golden Frequency of Abundance - Law of Attraction Music,

1111Hz: Spiritual Love and Angelic Energy Healing: frequency meditation music.

What is the hidden knowledge of vibration? All energy transmits in different frequencies. The power of vibration can destroy, as seen in earthquakes, volcanoes, and the walls of Jericho in biblical times.

Pythagoras connected mathematics to sound and music, different vibration and frequency, music of the spheres.

In the 1920s, Doctor Royal Raymond Rife developed the Rife Frequency Generator machines. An electro-magnetic radio transmitting low frequency waves. It was used on experimental rats, which had developed cancerous tumours, introduced by man. They were cured.

In 1934, a US team led by a Doctor Johnson convinced 16 terminally ill cancer patients from a Santiago Hospital to undergo sound frequency treatment, in a special clinic set up for the experiment over 90 days. The cure took place over 70 days for the first 14 patients, and the other 2 were cured within the 90 day period. The frequency to cancel cancer cells between 100,000 Hz to 400,000 Hz.

Why was this not approved for the treatment of cancer? It is against the financial interest of Banksters, Big Pharma, Doctors, and the Medical Profession, and the Satanists in the One World Government.

Sound Frequencies for the Human Body
There is a website with the above title that provides valuable information on sound frequencies for the human body. These frequencies are created within an electromagnetic field to produce enhanced music tones.
With the right equipment, valuable healing can be attained, but with the FDA at war against Homeopathic medicine, it will be interesting times in the Courts ahead.

It is known that 40 Hz reduces Alzheimer's, depression, sleep disorders, and other illnesses. Sadly, the technology threatens Big Pharma, and the Medical Profession are compliant. The good news is that "Medbeds" developed by Nicola Tesla, patent stolen and withheld by FBI, are now being manufactured, and will be available in 2023.

Hopefully, this will contribute to the bankruptcy of Big Pharma, as well as the legal cases stacking up for crimes against humanity, war profiteering and murder of mRNA vaccine patients, for a vaccine that is not fit for purpose.
We also have to include the Governments of the day being complicit, and the Medical Profession being compliant, and losing their integrity.

"They will have nothing, and they will be happy"
We all dream!

TESLA 3 – 6 – 9: VORTEX MATHS

Visualisation in the most simplistic terms
Is this the key to the Universe?

Divide 1 by 7 always produces 142857 the spare key to the universe, if you lost the master copy?

The Vortex
Take a circle and divide it into 9 with the nine at the top, followed by 1 as in a clock.

It leads to a mathematical heart curve, and many more that are too complex to demonstrate here.

Join 1 to 5, 5 to 7, 7 to 8, 8 to 4, 4 to 2, and 2 to 1. You are left with the Tesla vortex, 3, 6, and 9 numbers not touched.

Multiply the joined up numbers by 2, doubling each number.

DIGITAL ROOTS

DIGITAL ROOTS

1	**=**		**= 1**
2	**=**		**= 2**
4	**=**		**= 4**
8	**=**		**= 8**
16	**= 1+6**		**= 7**
32	**= 3+2**		**= 5**
64	**= 6+4**	**=10 = 1+0**	**= 1**
128	**= 1+2+8**	**= 11 = 1+1**	**= 2**
256	**= 2+5+6**	**= 13 = 1+3**	**= 4**
512	**= 5+1+2**		**= 8**
1024	**= 1+0+2+4**	**= 7**	**= 7**
2048	**= 2+0+4+8**	**=14 = 1+4**	**= 5**

Repeats in perpentuity.

Digital Roots in reverse

1		= 1
0.5		= 5
0.25		= 7
0.125		= 8
0.0625 = 13	=1+3	= 4
0.03125 = 11	= 1+1	= 2
0.015625 = 19 =1+9 =10=1+0		= 1
0.0078125 = 23	= 2+3	= 5
0.00390625 = 25	= 2+5	= 7
0.001953125 = 26	= 2+6	= 8
0.0009765625 = 4		
0.00048828125 = 2		

Repeats in reverse in perpetuity.

Teslas Numbers 3, 6, and 9 not visited.

The Vortex 3 and 6

3	= 3	3	=3
6	= 6	1.5	=6

12	**= 3**	**0.75**	**=3**
24	**= 6**	**0.375**	**=6**
48	**= 3**	**0.1875**	**=3**
96	**= 6**	**0.09375**	**=6**
192	**= 3**	**0.046875**	**=3**
384	**= 6**	**0.0234375**	**=6**
768	**= 3**	**0.01171875**	**=3**

The Vortex 9's

9 = 9

18 = 9

36 = 9

72 = 9

144 = 9

288 = 18 = 1 + 8 = 9

576 = 18 = 1 + 8 = 9

The above can easily be understood, it can be scaled up or down into considerably more complex diagrams and designs. Best left to the mathematicians and designers obsessed with maths.

What was the point of adding the consuming mystery of 3-6-9 which was so important to Tesla?

We are dealing with a civilisation of eight billion souls on this planet Earth now. How do the Elites and Oligarch's control the world population? Employing and using proxy forces to enforce the New World Disorder.

Civilisation can be divided into two parts, ninety nine percent human, and one percent inhuman.

Let us analyse the inhuman element, the zero point zero zero one percent (0.001%), or 8 million people who are attempting to control the world. it is speculative but it must exist in some form or another.

World Elites and Oligarchs Management Team
300 = 0.0000375%
World Elites and Oligarchs
7,700 = 0.0009625%
Politicians in 214 countries
214 x 250 average = 53,500 = 0.0066875%
Company Executives in 214 Countries
214 x 400 average = 85,600 = 0.0107%
Operatives
214 x 200 average = 42,800 = 0.00535%
Deep State

214 x 1,200 average = 256,800 = 0.0321%
Totally Aware Individuals
Above added together = 446,700 = 0.0558375%

Add to the above the blind supporters, Police, Armed Forces who have been corrupted with the threat of bullying, bribes, blackmail, and large financial rewards.

Probably unaware, but definitely controlled through the edict of command.

Blind supporters =7,553,300 = 0.9441625%

Thus One Percent of the world population can with careful planning, and good communications, control the plan, amend the plan, through the total control of the media and propaganda, and the total ignorance of an unsuspecting population.

Each Elite, or Oligarch only needs to communicate;
With less than 7 politicians.
With less than 11 company executives
With less than 5 Operatives
With less than 33 Deep State Operatives.

Total 56 people to contact for each Elite/Oligarch to mobilize the New World Disorder.

I imagine it is more sophisticated than I have demonstrated, but well within the capabilities of ruthless men and women, as we are beginning to realise.

ADVANCES IN SCIENCE AND TECHNOLOGY TO HELP MANKIND

We must throw away the dogma of corrupt science, controlled by corrupt financiers, and open our minds to alternative science. This was known by our distant forebears, but forgotten through catastrophic earth events, causing loss of man's position, followed by mass amnesia of the past. Some of this science, however, is not lost, it exists in the minds of the tribes with no written language, the information being handed down from generation to generation.

The energy of sound frequency and vibration was used to cut stone in Egyptian times, but probably much before that.

A Swede doctor, Dr Yarrow, studied in Oxford with a Tibetan student in the 1930s. In 1939, The English Scientific Society invited Dr Yarrow to Egypt. Whilst there, a friend of his Tibetan friend from his University days, invited him to visit Tibet to treat the Tibetan Lama of the day.
Dr Yarrow learned a lot on his visit, he was invited to attend a levitation event. The item to be raised was a stone slab 1 metre x 1.5 metre x 0.15 m thick. The block of stone had to be lifted 250 metres up a cliff face, to the entrance to a cave in the face of the vertical cliff using only sound.

How was it done?

There were 25 Tibetan Monks, 6 with trumpets, and 19 with drums. They were positioned in a semicircle with the stone in the centre, positioned 250 metres away from the cliff face. The Monks, by chanting, singing, imparting prayer, and playing the drums, and trumpets, slowly raised the stone by levitation to its required position. The Monks accessed the cave down a rope ladder from the top of the cliff.

All this was captured on film by Dr Yarrow, but the English Society who had sponsored Dr Yarrow confiscated the two films made of the event.

The assembling of the pyramids around the world are now easily explained by the known technology of the day, forgotten by humanity but still in use in the Tibetan culture, using sound vibration techniques.

The West has proved the above in the laboratory, but with small objects. If western man's achievements are greater than that it is being kept secret and withheld from mankind.

TESLA WARDENCLIFFE TOWER 1901

This was a wireless transmission tower located in Shoreham, New York, and was at the heart of Nicola Tesla's desire to provide free electricity for mankind.

The tower structure was completed, but J.P. Morgan withdrew funding for Tesla to complete the project. J.P Morgan owned many Power stations and was not interested in free power for the deplorables.

At that time, the economy was in a bubble, and speculative bubbles were bursting. The investors lost confidence in Tesla's brilliance.

Tesla had worked out that the earth's electric voltage gradient:
at ground level is 0 volts
at 1.00 metre high is 100 volts
at 2.00 metres high is 200 volts
at 10.00 metres high is 1,000 volts
at 100.00 metres high is 10,000 volts.

It is thought that Tesla got his idea from the Great Pyramid of Giza, and only now are scientists looking at Giza in a new light.

The latest speculative thinking regarding the Great Pyramid of Giza is it was a water magnetron microwave oscillator, which operated within the granite quarts rock of the pyramid. It has been suggested that it is a torsion energy generator, which would make a trumpet like noise.

WHAT CAN MAN DO TO HELP HIMSELF?

Man/woman is the master/mistress of his/her mind, and the mentor of his/her body.

Self-healing is within all man and woman's capabilities.
Why are we ill? The physical and spiritual body are one and the same. As we draw into the new crystalline 5 dimensional world, we need to reduce our food intake.
Go organic with fruit and vegetables, eaten raw rather than cooking the goodness out of it.
Genetically modified, processed food, and starch should be avoided. Sadly, no alcohol and tobacco, so these industries will suffer if man decides to take his health destiny into his own hands.

There is a need for truthful information to be given, and Doctors released from control by Big Pharma financial incentives. There should be an independent council to report bad medicine, which is empowered to impose financial sanction against the companies creating the ill health result, and financing Lawfare against good medicine.

Doctors need to retrain to provide simple health solutions that do not rely on big pharma expensive drugs, but rather, spend more time learning of food allergy and how the various foods affect the body, and create illness.

My understanding is that doctors spend one week of their training in lectures relating to food at University.

Histamine Intolerance is treated by giving anti-histamine pills. The reality is, by eating correctly and omitting the histamine inducing foods, the problem goes away, and the need to take pills no longer applies. How many more home remedies make the doctor redundant?

Sadly, the doctor would be unable to answer the correct foods to eat.

It is recognised that gluten intolerance can be treated by eating correctly for that individual, which may not apply to others.

Cochrane an investigative body, which advises the World Health Organisation, a cabal organisation recognised that carbo hydrates contained no nutrients; for example rice, corn, wheat and processed foods.

"There is insufficient evidence from randomised controlled trials to date to recommend consumption of whole grain diets to reduce the risk of cardiovascular disease, or lower blood cholesterol or blood pressure."
The above sets off a forest fire in the body – inflammation.

It elevates blood sugar, which elevates insulin. Calories flow into fat, but do not flow out. It leads to Alzheimer's.
Better foods would be vegetables and fruit in their raw state, kale, and spinach, dark leafy greens, avocados every day, lots of eggs, and red meat in moderation. Salmon, and sardines for the brain cells.
To maintain a low insulin state fasting should become a regular activity.

The Journal of Alzheimer's Association recommends a high intake of foods with a high glycaemic load, whether as fruit, or as highly refined carbohydrates, may disrupt insulin signalling, impair glucose metabolism, and thereby contribute to neuronal loss, reduced cortical thickness, and cognitive impairment.

Extra virgin olive oil is a robust risk reducer for Alzheimer's.

THE FUTURE FOR MANKIND

What is the Soul?
Birth right of the soul is free will.

Each of us possess a soul, or spirit which occupies our body during life on earth, but abandoning our body on death. All religions of the world have believed this since time began. We are the living product of several or many lives at once. We just cannot remember the previous lives in this one, and the influence they are having on this life.

No life is ever finished. We can look forward to being reborn in a different time and place with many of the souls we know today and in past lives being with us in a new lifetime with a new identity, all influenced by the sins of our past lives.

Mankind is currently in a state of hypnotised unconsciousness, which we have suffered all our lives.
Divine consciousness has to be our ultimate desire.

Grief, the five stages we undergo.

1. Denial
2. Bargaining Phase
3. Anger
4. Depression
5. Acceptance

Disclosure of the truth has been happening for thousands of years, but non-disclosure of truth is also true.

The earth is in the midst of a New Earth Ascension Process. The Mayan Calendar has come to an end with this Winter Solstice on the 21st of December 2022.

What can we expect from this change?

The earth's enhanced frequency electro magnetic resonance is the same as nuclear weapons, suggesting these nuclear weapons are neutralised?

We can expect that man's collective consciousness and raised spirituality will affect his future behaviour.

We can expect changes to the global energy fields affecting earth, everyone and everything on it.

We can expect changes in weather patterns to be more extreme, recognising the dead sun's influence on the sun, moon and earth.

We can expect changes in the political leadership, as new nations develop, and corruption is purged from the world's governments, industry, and influence pedlars.

We can expect a change, an enormous lift in our DNA, from 2 strand, 3 dimension, to 4 strand, 4 dimension and 5 strand, 5 dimension DNA development in line with the Earth's Ascension Process, which affects the animals too.

This shift has commenced, and will continue into 2023 and 2024. The human race must prepare for this enormous enhancement to their physical and spiritual uplift by GOD.

There is going to be a rise in good energy and a fall in negative energy after the 21st of December Solstice, 2022.
This will fill all of the peoples on earth's minds.

There will be an activation of Chakra of all human beings, and their 3rd eye, their pineal gland, will look beyond physical to a spiritual domain, as too will the animals who share our earth.

A coming together of the Material and Spiritual domain will change to a higher level of awareness of the human race.

The human population are going to have a direct connection, via their pineal gland to infinite knowledge.

The world economy is moving from a global economy to a regional de-globalised economy centred round the individual country in survival mode. Each country's treasures, like the N.H.S., priceless properties, and assets will be sold off to the Oligarchs' and big business to fund the Government and the Banks. Police and the Armed Services will be maintained to protect the Government in Power.

In the words of Klaus Schwab, "**you will have nothing and you will be happy**". Turn that statement upside down, "the Oligarchs, Corrupt Governments, and Big Business will have nothing, and we will be happy."

FUBAR – Fucked up beyond all recognition/repair.

The future, being introduced by the World Economic Forum, aims to cripple our world. We need to awaken the world, disarm and remove the W.E.F. green missiles aimed at destroying farming, energy, food, so that they can control the population of the world absolutely.

We need to refuse the big Pharma vaccines against COVID, and other negative treatments introduced to make humanity permanently ill, to achieve the hybridisation of the human race to create a slave society.

The Prophecy of Edgar Cayce is not something I am going to disclose.

Trump did not sign the insurrection act. Reason? He wanted Biden and the Democratic/Republican Cabal to act out the W.E.F. plan for the economy, do as they wished. Trump's plan is to awaken the brainwashed people, but also it is GOD's plan to prevent a civil war.

The New American Republic is a new beginning for the world. The Democrats had to accelerate the W.E.F. plan, which Trump had unravelled while President from 2016 to 2020. This caused the WEF to awaken the American people. The mind control programming of the world population is being reversed, as the release of truth slowly awakens the people over several years. Lies have been taught as truth all our lives.

The reverse is true – truth has been taught as lies all our lives.

Short-term, we must eradicate the cancerous Satanic growth that has captured mankind, and brainwashed the population at the moment. There is hope, because many corrupt politicians are resigning, or running away worldwide, because of a rebelling population.

The French Revolution comes to mind, where the guillotines were much in use.

We can expect worldwide political unrest whilst the transition happens. Hopefully, man will enter a 1,000 years of peace after the transition.

The government has to devolve power back to the people, by increasing the role of local councils, and make the population more responsible for their environment.
Also, break up international organisations and companies.
They seek to monopolise power and manipulate governments. If power is devolved, these companies lose the ability to control power as it is micromanaged.

Many multi-national companies are bigger than the countries they operate in, bully and bribe the government representatives to avoid responsibility for pollution, non-payment of taxes and royalty fees due to the country.

Long-term, man must adapt, but with 6,000 patents withheld from humanity for in many cases over 70 years, man's progress has been held back by control and greed. These patents include free energy devices, water engines, instead of petrol.

All these patents have been stolen by the F.B.I., on behalf of the Black Hat Cabal represented by the One World Government, New World Order, and World Economic Forum.
There is an:
Illusion of the supremacy of hate and fear over love.
Belief in the supremacy of dark over light.

We need to awaken the world to getting back to a new normal, drive the world economy forward with new eco-friendly technologies. Disarm fear and propaganda, and speak out against corruption.

That will truly happen when the Great Solar Flash takes place to awaken all of mankind to GOD's presence. There will be a period of two to three days of sleep to acclimatise to your new body's capabilities, to recover from the flash. Many people will become psychic, telepathic and a veil of forgetfulness will be lifted from your mind.

Animals will be able to communicate with mankind.

WHAT DIMENSIONS DO WE LIVE IN?

Lower chakras expose us to the physical, the ability to see, and smell physically.

Ascension is taking place in the earth we live in. This is a spiritualisation of the earth, integration of the spirit and matter. The veil is going to be lifting, the individual's Akashic records will be available. This records all your previous life experiences.

The human DNA is a bio hard drive that collects all your thoughts and activity, and transmits to the Creator GOD, and records your last fourteen generations of memories in your DNA which are withheld from our consciousness.

Beware of the dark negative energy, which seeks to overwhelm your mind. We, with our 3 dimension capabilities, operate at 4% capacity, with 2 strand DNA.

Superpowers are possible with enhanced 4 and 5 strand DNA.

The upgrade DNA downloads are coming from our future beings on another dimension. Your previous lost and hidden memories will return.

3rd dimension, height, width, depth, – man can look, our DNA, 40Hz is the dream state of the human body in sleep.
3rd density 100% physical.

4th dimension, Tara Earth, height, width, depth, time and space:
4th density is 75% physical, and 25% spiritual.
Time travel in the past; and the future is possible.
Man can look, with 4th dimension enhanced DNA.
Not everyone will be receptive to moving up from the 3rd dimension to the 4th and 5th dimension.
More sensitive to love.
Space-time is Einstein's Theory of Relativity, gravitational waves proved in 2015.

5th dimension, Tara Earth, ascension spirit, memory in the soul, enhanced DNA. Everybody will be more psychic, telepathic, have sympathy with mother earth.
5th density is 50% physical, and 50% spiritual.
Goldilocks zone. We think at the speed of light, and we can fly.

Your inner voice is from the 5th dimension.
Internal monologue is the voice in your head.

Specific brain mechanism developed in childhood. You do not have to talk to think.
Your eyes do not see your future, but you can see in your mind your past. See your past and your future without opening your eyes. Electrical energy in your body.

This is a time when you can interpret what other people are thinking through telepathy. A time when learning silence is wise, as nobody likes to have their thoughts interpreted, and a reply follows from a stranger.

Highest level of discernment
High frequencies experiencing the golden age of miracles.

6th dimension; Tara Earth
7th dimension; Gaia Earth
8th dimension; Gaia Earth
9th dimension; Gaia Earth
10th dimension; Aramatina Earth
11th dimension; Aramatina Earth
12th dimension; Aramatina Earth
Arctuarians are 12th dimensional with a 24 strand DNA;

Above the 12th dimension, Sophia Earth is pure light force.

Archangel Meditron is an example, all angels are 13th dimension upwards to the 15th dimension.

What is GOD's Spirit?

I am light, I am love, I am truth, I am.

What is Man/Woman's Spirit?
LOVE

A man/woman's dimension is the vibrational frequency of his/her body.

Man/woman is self is a three dimensional being on the physical plane.
EMOTION

Man/woman is carbon based with a 2 DNA Strand

Man/woman is self is a four dimensional being on the astral plane.
FEELING

Man/woman is crystalline based with a 12 DNA Strand
Man/woman is self is a five dimensional being on the light body plane
LOVE IS ALL THERE IS.

Your Guardian or Spirit is your heart, and is ruled by your emotions, love, and many negative emotions emanating from your mind. Three-dimensional consciousness must be trained in your higher self. Previous incarnations are not necessarily on this earth.

Your imagination is actually from your previous memories from past lives, of 3rd, 4th, and 5th dimensional experiences. Your heart controls your higher self, and many people permit their lives to be controlled by their minds, (imprisoned) and not their hearts, perhaps out of fear.

This is reflected in man's desire for perpetual wars throughout the world. This tactic employs deception to trap the innocent, and imprison their minds in destructive behaviour.

Man must become the master of his mind, and not the servant of another mind. Man must become the guardian of his heart, and dedicate his life to helping others.

There are beings with up to 15 dimensions. It is suggested that there are at least 5 parallel earths, and we all have doppelgangers, they are us in these parallel worlds.

Atlantis, and Limeira exist on Terra Earth, in the 5th dimension where extinct species return. The planet will be much bigger, four times the size. We will grow taller, up to 2 feet!

Civilisation has been on earth for millions of years. Dinosaurs were meat eaters, so were decimating the human race, and had to be destroyed. The species was developed by Reptilians, and got out of control. God rebalanced the earth to be free of them.

The Mayan Calendar was created from the Atlantis Calendar. Our modern day Calendar is a Cabal Calendar, which is approximately ten years out of adjustment.
Artificial intelligence is controlled by the Cabal, but that too is controlled by a stronger negative force. The Beast in the Bible is Artificial Intelligence.

The world awaits disclosure, and the energising of the Emergency Broadcast System (EBS). Without the White Hats re-establishing control, the human race would be under much stronger control by the

Black Hats. These criminals are being arrested at one thousand a day in America, and it will take more than a year to complete the task. The problem similarly exists in all countries of the world.

Those in the $7^{th,}$ 8th and 9th dimensions can live on the sun. They are many millions of years ahead of us.

There is a Japanese Proverb that a fish rots from the head down. Corruption starts from the top down, the King starts the rot. The King's Commanders are quick to exploit, and extend the rot.

In today's world, substitute Elites for Kings, the rot is the same.

In today's world, substitute Corporations for Kings, the rot is the same.

In today's world, substitute Governments for Kings, the rot is the same.

In today's world, substitute Deep State for Kings, the rot is the same.

The common man/woman pays the price of corruption with taxes, more taxes, more taxes, and then death, which he has to pay for too!

Humanity is fighting a war of survival against Satanic Forces. We must chose faith over fear, and ignore the illusion projected by Satanists, and their servants.

The following is a poem I wrote for my son on the 30th of March 1993.

OPEN YOUR MIND

Open your mind to:
The life we learn, of false values,
Money materialism and power,
And the life we live, of false morality,
Bigotry, selfishness and hostility,
And empty your mind.

Is your mind unconscious?
Or, is your mind conscious?
Are you surrounded by truth?
Or, submerged in untruth?
Deception is illusion is an unconscious mind.
Open your mind.

Experience the birth of self-awareness,
Of irrationality the enemy within,
There are things which cause you to lose,
Your reason, or have you none to lose?
To ever widening freedom and responsibility,
Open your mind.

To the pursuit of knowledge,
The crisis of adolescence,
The struggles, the choices, and advances,
From familiar, to unfamiliar,
To ever widening freedom and responsibility,

Open your mind.

To the uncertainty of time,
Teaching us the most important lesson of all,
To integrate with humanity,
By expression of unconditional love,
And live by meaning which we choose,
Open your mind.

That the ultimate criteria are,
The honesty, integrity, courage and love,
Of a given moment of relatedness,
With those special friends,
To whom hurt would kill the joy,
Open your mind.

If we have it,
We can trust the future to itself,
The heart has its reasons,
That reason knows not of,
Is it in your heart to:
Open your mind.

To your own dream land,
Intuition your Inquisitor,
Imagination your salvation,
To the love of Jesus, the son,
Lord God, the Father, and the Holy Spirit,

Open your mind.

The Power of Prayer to Our Lord will overwhelm Satan, and his Worshippers. Now I have to leave that task to my readers.

The power of poetry is insurmountable, and I add a poem that I found. The writer is I believe John Greenleaf Whittier, 1807 – 1892, but the wording is slightly different from his poem. It sends a very strong message to your spirit, no matter how bad it gets, do not quit.

DON'T QUIT

When things go wrong as they sometimes will;
When the road you're trudging seems all uphill;
When funds are low and the debts are high
And you want to smile but you have to sigh;
When care is pressing you down a bit,
Rest, if you must, but don't you quit.

Life is strange with its twists and turns
As every one of us sometimes learns,
And many a failure comes about
When they might have won had they stuck it out.
Don't give up though the pace seems slow,
And you may succeed with another blow.

Success is failure turned inside out,
God's hidden gift in the clouds of doubt.
And you never can tell how close you are,
It may be near when it seems so far.
So stick to the fight when you're hardest hit.
It's when things seem worst
That you must not quit.

For all the sad words of tongue and pen
The saddest are these "It might have been"

I awakened late after a powerful dream, to a new day.
My spirit is uplifted in the knowledge that JESUS CHRIST is on my side.

ERRORS AND OMISSIONS EXEMPTED

A DREAM BY WILLIAM WALLACE.

ABOUT THE AUTHOR

William Dingwall was born and grew up in Stirling. Throughout his life, he has resided in South Africa, Botswana, Dover and Saudi Arabia, until eventually moving back to Stirling to look after his mum and siblings. The Author enjoys the simple things in life such as gardening, DIY work, and seasonal chutney and jam making. He has two children who currently reside in Harrogate and Leeds respectively. He did not intend to write a book when he first began writing, and the Author's inspiration and motivation, came from a current affairs group in U3A which he joined in May 2022, when he began exchanging views with other members about different topics – the most prominent subject of which being global warming. *What Happened When I Was Asleep* is his first book.

SELECT BIBLIOGRAPHY

Sources of Information and facts:

Message from the Mehbians – goldenageofgaia.com Nov 16, 2021, Various others on Google
Black Knight Satellite – gaia.com, Google, Wikipedia
Sumerian Tablets – Paul Wallis author of "Escape from Eden"
Admiral Pirie Reis born 1465 – Google, Wikipedia
Orenteus Finaeus Map 1531 – Google, Wikipedia, Charles Hapgood. USA 8th Reconnaissance Technical Squadron (SAC)
Captain John Davis 1821 – Google, Wikipedia.
Operation High Jump – Wikipedia, Britannica, Smithsonian, YouTube, south-pole.com, cgaviationhistory.org, medium.com, galnet.fandom.com, coolantartica.com
Aliens Off Planet – Ismael Perez author of "Our Cosmic Origins"
Aliens Inner Earth – Baba Vanga, Pat Price, Gene Decode, https://youtu.be/jNqYXJAzjOU,
Majic12 – Robertspaceindustries.com, wolfbane.com

Google, YouTube.

President Kennedy – Wikipedia, YouTube Dr Robert McClelland, Zapruder Film Mystery

Barry Soetoro – Google, Servando Gonzalez, Author

The Earth, sun, moon, etc – Google, YouTube.

Pioneer 10 & 11 – Google, YouTube.

Georgia Guidestones – Google, YouTube.

Nesara/Gesara – Charlie Ward, YouTube

God's Prophets – Amanda Grace, Julie Green, Rebekah Erland, Robin & Robyn Bullock, Timothy Dixon, Hank Kunneman, Kent Christmas, Mario Murillo, Perry Stone, Troy Black, on YouTube.

Music Hz – YouTube

Vortex Maths – YouTube

Advances in Science – YouTube

Mankind Future – Marshall Vian Summers author "The Allies of Humanity," Ismael Perez author "Our Cosmic Origins"

Electric Price Scam – Yanis Varoufakis

Pope Benedict XV1 – Dr Taylor Marshall